Mexican Spanish for Beginners

Your Guide to Speaking and Understanding the Language and Culture of Mexico with Confidence

© Copyright 2024 - All rights reserved.

The content contained within this book may not be reproduced, duplicated, or transmitted without direct written permission from the author or the publisher.

Under no circumstances will any blame or legal responsibility be held against the publisher, or author, for any damages, reparation, or monetary loss due to the information contained within this book, either directly or indirectly.

Legal Notice:

This book is copyright protected. It is only for personal use. You cannot amend, distribute, sell, use, quote, or paraphrase any part, or the content within this book, without the consent of the author or publisher.

Disclaimer Notice:

Please note the information contained within this document is for educational and entertainment purposes only. All effort has been executed to present accurate, up-to-date, reliable, and complete information. No warranties of any kind are declared or implied. Readers acknowledge that the author is not engaging in the rendering of legal, financial, medical, or professional advice. The content within this book has been derived from various sources. Please consult a licensed professional before attempting any techniques outlined in this book.

By reading this document, the reader agrees that under no circumstances is the author responsible for any losses, direct or indirect, that are incurred as a result of the use of the information contained within this document, including, but not limited to, errors, omissions, or inaccuracies.

Free Bonuses from Cecilia Melero

Hi Spanish Learners!

My name is Cecilia Melero, and first off, I want to THANK YOU for reading my book.

Now you have a chance to join my exclusive Spanish language learning email list so you can get the ebooks below for free as well as the potential to get more Spanish books for free! Simply click the link below to join.

P.S. Remember that it's 100% free to join the list.

Access your free bonuses here:
https://livetolearn.lpages.co/mexican-spanish-for-beginners-paperback/

Table of Contents

INTRODUCTION 1
BEFORE ARRIVING 3
SIMPLE GUIDE TO SPANISH PRONUNCIATION 4
LUNES: HELLO, MY FRIEND 10
MARTES: HOME SWEET HOME 25
MIÉRCOLES: FAMILY TREE 37
JUEVES: FOOD FOR DAYS 53
VIERNES: AROUND THE CITY 60
SÁBADO: FIELD TRIP 72
DOMINGO: THE LAST DAY 87
TIME TO GO HOME 100
ANSWER KEY 108
CONCLUSION 114
HERE'S ANOTHER BOOK BY LINGO PUBLISHING THAT YOU MIGHT LIKE 119
FREE BONUSES FROM CECILIA MELERO 120

Introduction

¡Hola! Welcome to this Mexican Spanish coursebook for beginners. If you are reading this, three things are true:
- #1: you are not from Mexico
- #2: you don't know how to speak Spanish
- And #3: **you just made the best decision of your life!**

"How so?" you may ask. Well, Spanish is one of the most important languages on Earth. This opinion may seem a bit biased, but let's look at the facts: as the mother tongue of nearly 493 million people, **Spanish has more than 591 million speakers around the world.** Additionally, it is the third most widely used language on the Internet and the official language of 21 countries. This means there are many different Spanish accents you could have chosen to learn.

But no, you chose to learn the variant of the people from Mexico, which has one of the largest Spanish-speaking populations in the world. This means that you will be able to communicate with around 125 million Spanish speakers!

This is not a thing to be taken lightly. In fact, this Mexican Spanish course is so keen for you to learn to communicate that **it has designed its entire structure around that goal,** a structure different from that of traditional coursebooks. Why? Because this book will take you on **an immersion Spanish trip to Mexico!**

Yes, that's right: pack your bags as you follow **George Donovan**, a young man from the United States, throughout the course of his **week-**

long summer vacation in Mexico City. You will be his companion during the entire book, from the moment he lands to the day he heads back home. Each day of this awesome trip is a chapter filled with Spanish grammar content, vocabulary, and exercises to practice what you've learned.

Hand in hand with George, you'll discover all the wonders the Mexican language and culture have to offer. But he won't be the only person you'll meet on this Spanish journey: **Paula Solís, George's long-time friend and Spanish teacher,** will be there to guide you both with simple explanations, clear examples, and even jokes! This local guide will take George (and yourself) around the city's tourist landmarks and pristine beaches – and will even open the doors of her own family home.

That's not all: because this is a Mexican Spanish course, there's a **cultural annex** at the end of every chapter, each filled with specific slang, idioms, and fun facts. You'll also learn the differences between this dialect and Castilian Spanish. With this extra knowledge, you'll become a local in no time, and your new Mexican friends will celebrate your interest in their homeland.

It's time you join George and begin your Mexican-Spanish journey. ¡Ándale!

Before Arriving

As I laid back on my seat with an open bag of complimentary peanuts in my hand, I enjoyed the view from above the clouds. Three hours ago, I, George Donovan, hopped on a plane from Los Angeles with a single destination in mind: Mexico City. My good friend Paula, whom I had met some years earlier, had invited me to visit her in her hometown.

At first, I had my doubts. I had never left my country, so it was natural to feel a bit nervous. Besides that, the language barrier also worried me, as Spanish was not my strong suit... Well, right until that trip, that was. Truthfully, I didn't even know how to say "hello" at the time! Paula was well aware of my struggles with the language, so she was so kind as to volunteer to be my private Spanish tutor while I visited Mexico. I couldn't refuse such an opportunity!

When I agreed, she got down to work and sent me an email attachment with some warm-up material for me to read while I was on the plane. It was a PDF file about Spanish pronunciation, which I downloaded before take-off. The file was incredibly organized: she was a certified Spanish teacher for a reason. With over one hour left on my flight, I opened the file on my tablet and started reading. This is what I learned from Paula's guide:

Simple Guide to Spanish Pronunciation

Before going straight to phonetics, Paula told me that not only do English and Spanish sound different but there are also *different Spanish accents out there*. However, she would focus on that variety because I wanted to learn Spanish from Mexico.

Vowel Sounds

First, I learned the vowel sounds. Luckily for me, Paula said that while English has between fifteen and twenty vowel sounds (depending on the dialect), **Spanish has only five.** This means that each vowel has only one pronunciation. Paula had made a table with them: in the pronunciation column, the words were separated into syllables by a hyphen and with the stressed syllable underlined. This was the table:

Vowel	Sounds like English...	Example	Pronunciation
A	ah	**a**rte	<u>ahr</u>-teh
E	eh	**e**co	<u>eh</u>-koh
I	ee	**i**dea	<u>ee</u>-deh-ah

| O | oh | color | koh-<u>lohr</u> |
| U | oo | m<u>ú</u>sica | <u>moo</u>-see-kah |

Then, Paula mentioned that there are only two cases where vowels change their pronunciation depending on the letters around them. Both cases involve the same vowels, so they were easy for me to remember: **whenever UE and UI are preceded by a Q or a G, the U is silent.** Paula wrote some examples for me to check:

Vowel	Sounds like English...	Example	Pronunciation
QUE	keh	queso	<u>keh</u>-soh
QUI	kee	quince	<u>keen</u>-sehn
GUE	geh	guerra	<u>geh</u>-rrah
GUI	gee	guía	<u>gee</u>-ah

Consonant Sounds

After that, I moved over to consonants. I found them to be a little bit trickier, but Paula kept her explanation simple by starting with the similar ones:

- Spanish B is like English B, but we let out less air when pronouncing it
- D is pronounced the same in both languages
- F is pronounced the same in both languages
- K is pronounced the same in both languages
- Spanish M is pronounced just like English
- Spanish N is also pronounced like the English N
- L is pronounced the same in both languages
- Spanish P is like the English P, but we let out less air when pronouncing it.S is pronounced the same in both languages

- Spanish T is like English T, but we let out less air when we pronounce it
- W is pronounced the same in both languages, but it's not frequently used in Spanish

Then, I checked the ones that are a bit different – but still quite easy:
- Spanish Q is pronounced like English K
- Consonants B and V are both pronounced like the English B
- In Mexican Spanish, Z is pronounced like S. However, in Spain, Z has a sound similar to English TH in "think"
- In Spanish, H is always silent
- J is pronounced like the H in "hello"
- Ñ is the only Spanish letter that doesn't exist in English. (Paula gave a very cool tip: its pronunciation is similar to the combination NY in the name Kanye).

So far, so good. Sadly, the most challenging ones followed:
- In Spanish, LL is called *doble ele* (i.e., "double L"), and its pronunciation varies depending on the region. In Mexico, it's pronounced like the Y in "you" or the J in "jello."
- Y is also pronounced differently depending on the region. It's pronounced like LL in Mexico, except when it's on its own or at the end of a word. In these cases, Y is pronounced like a Spanish I.
- There are four possible pronunciations for C:
    o Before A, O, and U, it sounds like English K
    o Before E and I, it sounds like English S
    o The CH combination is pronounced like CH in "chocolate"
    o The CC combination is pronounced like KS
- G has two possible pronunciations:
    o Before A, O, U, or a consonant is pronounced softly, like G in "gas"
    o Before E and I, it is pronounced like H in "hello"
    o Before the combinations UE and UI, the U is silent, and the G is pronounced softly

- R has two possible pronunciations:
    - When R appears in the middle (especially between vowels) or at the end of a word, it's pronounced softly, like the TT of "better" in some American dialects, that is, like a regular English R, only with the tongue closer to the front of the mouth, touching the ridge behind the upper teeth.
    - When R appears at the beginning of a word or when there is a double R, it's pronounced strongly. This sound is called "rolled R." To pronounce it, I had to place my tongue in the ridge behind my upper teeth and make a trill between my tongue and that bone. It was pretty hard, honestly, but then I got it!
- Finally, X has three possible pronunciations. I panicked when I read this, but Paula told me not to worry because it's not a very common consonant in Spanish.
    - At the beginning of words, it's pronounced like S
    - In the middle or end of a word, it's pronounced like English X in "box"
    - In words like *México*, *Oaxaca*, and *Texas*, the X is pronounced like Spanish J, that is, like the H in "hot." So, Tay-Hahs, for "Texas."

At the end of this explanation, I checked the following chart with an example of each consonant:

Consonant	Sounds like English...	Example	Pronunciation
B, V	b	**b**ravo	**brah**-boh
C, Q, K	k	**qui**osco **k**ilo	**keeohs**-koh **kee**-loh
C, S, X	s	**c**entral **s**imple **x**ilofón	sehn-**trahl** **seem**-pleh see-loh-**fohn**
CH	ch	**ch**ef	chef

Consonant	Sounds like English...	Example	Pronunciation
D	d	**d**ata	**dah**-tah
F	f	**f**atal	fah-**tal**
G	g	**g**lobal	gloh-**bahl**
G, J, X	h	**g**eneral **j**ungla Mé**x**ico	heh-neh-**rahl** **hoon**-glah **meh**-hee-koh
H	silent	**h**otel	oh-**tehl**
L	l	**l**ocal	loh-**kahl**
LL, Y	y, j	**ll**ama **y**oga	**yah**-mah **yoh**-gah
M	m	**m**apa	**mah**-pah
N	n	**n**ota	**noh**-tah
Ñ	ny	se**ñ**al	seh-**nyahl**
P	p	**p**olicía	poh-lee-**see**-ah
R	tt, r	colo**r**	koh-**lohr**
RR	rr	**r**adio	**rah**-deeoh
T	t	**t**alento	tah-**lehn**-toh
W	w	ki**w**i	**kee**-wee

Consonant	Sounds like English...	Example	Pronunciation
X	x	te**x**to	teh**x**-toh
Y	ee	jerse**y**	**y**ehr-sehee

And that was all Paula told me I needed to know about Mexican Spanish pronunciation *for now*. At the end, she wrote: "I recommend you return to this PDF whenever you don't know how to say a word out loud."

Just when I finished reading Paula's file, I heard a voice through the plane's loudspeakers:

"Dear passengers, this is the captain speaking. We are about to land in Mexico City. Seat backs and tray tables must be placed in the upright position. **Please** fasten your seatbelts as we prepare for landing. **Thank you**."

Then, the voice from the captain said the same thing, but in Spanish:

"Señores pasajeros, les habla el capitán de este vuelo. Estamos a punto de aterrizar en Ciudad de México. Los respaldos de los asientos y las bandejas deben colocarse en posición vertical. **Por favor***, abróchense los cinturones mientras nos preparamos para el aterrizaje.* **Gracias***."*

At the time, I couldn't get any of the words, but I recognized some of the Spanish sounds Paula had taught me, which gave me hope. When I went back home a week later, I would understand every word. I looked out the window and saw Mexico City's urban landscape from above. I would never have guessed all the wonderful things the city had in store for me. In a matter of minutes, I would meet my friend Paula after a very long time.

Lunes: Hello, My Friend

After the turbulence stopped, I saw Mexico City from the ground for the first time. The moment I stepped out of the plane, a great heat wave hit me - a big contrast from the pressurized cabin. With a huge thrill, I went to the baggage claim area to pick up my luggage, and then I saw her: Paula was standing a few feet away from me, holding a paper sign that said "Georgie, the blond gringo" with a smiley face that echoed her facial features. I walked up to her and gave her a big hug. She kissed me on the cheek, something Latin American people do when they greet people.

"Hi, Georgie!" she said with that loud voice I remembered. "Did you like my sign?"

"I did," I answered laughing, "but I think only 'Georgie' would have sufficed."

"Nah, what's fun about that?" replied Paula. "Besides, you *are* a blond gringo. Are you ready to learn some Spanish?"

I was quite surprised to hear that question: Paula wasn't kidding around when she insisted on being my teacher. I hadn't even left the airport, and the Spanish immersion was about to begin!

As I hadn't had lunch yet, I was starving, so Paula suggested we sit down at a nice coffee shop inside the airport. We talked for a very long time about ourselves and what we had been up to these past couple of years. I was happy to see her; everything around me looked new and exciting! After catching up in English, we decided we could start with our first lesson. For starters, we covered the basics of saying "hello" and "goodbye" in Spanish. This is what I learned:

Greetings and Farewells

According to Paula, these are the most common ways to greet someone in Spanish:

- *hola* ("hello")
- *buenos días* ("good morning")
- *buen día* ("good day")
- *buenas tardes* ("good afternoon")
- *buenas noches* ("good evening" and "good night")
- *buenas* ("hey")
- *¡tanto tiempo!* ("it's been a long time!")
- *bienvenido* ("welcome," when you are addressing a man)
- *bienvenida* ("welcome," when you are addressing a woman)

Then, to ask about how someone is, she told me to say:

- *¿cómo estás?* ("how are you?" when you are addressing someone informally)
- *¿cómo está?* ("how are you?" when you are addressing someone formally)
- *¿qué tal?* ("how is it going?")

"How can I answer these questions?" I wondered. As if Paula had read my mind, she told me some possible answers:

- *bien, ¿y tú?* ("good, and you?" when you are addressing someone informally)
- *bien, ¿y usted?* ("good, and you?" when you are addressing someone formally)
- *muy bien, gracias* ("very well, thank you")
- *como siempre* ("same old")
- *regular* ("regular" / "not the best")
- *no muy bien* ("not very well")

Now, when the time has come to say goodbye, these are some common words and phrases:

- *adiós* ("goodbye")
- *adiosito* ("bye"; very common in Mexico)
- *chao* ("bye")

- *nos vemos* ("see you")
- *hasta mañana* ("see you tomorrow")
- *hasta luego* ("see you later")

My pronunciation wasn't the best, honestly, but I was happy to hear these phrases from a native speaker and, better yet, from my friend. When I finished eating, I walked with Paula to her car, where the lesson continued. This time, it was about personal pronouns! I was looking forward to it. Once we left the airport and entered the city, I was flabbergasted: Mexico City was much better than I had imagined. It is a huge city, with a lot of action and life. This is what I learned during the drive to my hotel:

Personal Pronouns

Subject personal pronouns are called *pronombres personales de sujeto* in Spanish. In Paula's technical words, "we use them instead of a noun in subject position when we've already mentioned the subject, or when it can be inferred from context." "But, what is the subject?" I asked her (I'm a mechanical engineer, so grammar is not my strong suit, not even in English). She told me the subject is the person or thing doing the *verb's action*. After I understood, Paula handed me a CHART (she had printed out a lot of Spanish materials just for me! I couldn't believe it) with the English personal pronouns and their Spanish counterparts so I could compare:

	English	Spanish
1st person singular	I	*Yo*
2nd person singular	You	*Tú*
		Usted
3rd person singular	He	*Él*
	She	*Ella*

1st person plural	We	*Nosotros*
		Nosotras
2nd person plural	You	*Ustedes*
3rd person plural	They	*Ellos*
		Ellas

Thankfully, I noticed both English and Spanish have three "persons." The first-person includes the speaker, the second-person includes the listener, and the third-person refers to someone or something outside the conversation. In turn, these three persons can be divided into singular and plural.

Paula made me notice that, in some cases, there is more than one Spanish pronoun for an English one. This was a bit confusing, but she explained each pronoun one by one and gave me an example with its corresponding translations:

First-person singular pronoun: *Yo* means "I." For example: *Yo soy Paula* ("I am Paula").

Second-person singular pronouns: *Tú* and *usted* mean "you" to refer to a single person, but they have different uses. *Tú* is the informal way of addressing someone, and although formality norms vary depending on social standards, this pronoun is generally used with people who are close to you and also used to address younger people. For example: *Tú eres rubio* ("You are blond").

Usted, on the other hand, is formal, and it's used with strangers, older people who are not close to you, or people in a position above you, such as bosses or teachers. For example: *Usted es americano* ("You are American").

Spanish has a third second-person singular pronoun, that is, equivalent to the singular "you." It's the pronoun *vos*. This pronoun is also used informally, like *tú*. However, lucky me, Paula told me that *vos* is only used in a couple of Southern Mexican states, so she said I shouldn't worry about it.

Third-person singular pronouns: *Él* means "he," and *ella* means "she." The distinction here is not related to register; just like in English, it is related to gender. *Él* is used as the masculine third-person singular pronoun: *Él es Martín* ("He is Martín"). *Ella* is the feminine third-person singular pronoun: *Ella es Clara* ("She is Clara").

First-person plural pronouns: *Nosotros* and *nosotras* both mean "we." "But if they both mean "we," then why do we have two pronouns in Spanish?" I asked Paula with the naivety of a beginner speaker. Well, she explained that, like with *él* and *ella*, there's a distinction in gender. *Nosotras* is the feminine first-person plural pronoun, and it's used to refer to a group of women or girls. For example: *Nosotras somos mujeres* ("We are women"). *Nosotros* is the masculine first-person plural pronoun, and it is used to refer to a group of men or boys. For example: *Nosotros somos chicos* ("We are boys"). When groups are made up of men and women, the masculine *nosotros* is used. This is called "generic masculine," and she said she would tell me more about it later. For example, if I said the phrase "We are friends" to talk about Paula and myself, it would be *Nosotros somos amigos,* even though Paula is a woman.

Second-person plural pronoun: *Ustedes* means "you" when we refer to more than one person. Paula told me to think of this pronoun as equivalent to "y'all," "youse" or "you guys." For example: *Ustedes son mexicanos* ("You guys are Mexican").

During her explanation, she stopped to clarify that there are two other second-person plural pronouns in Spanish: *vosotros* and *vosotras*. However, these two pronouns are only used in Spain, so she told me to forget about them while I stayed in Mexico!

Third-person plural pronouns: *Ellos* and *ellas* both mean "they." Ellos is the masculine third-person plural pronoun, and it is used to refer to a group of men or boys or a mixed-gender group. For example: *Ellos son muchos* ("They are many"). *Ellas* is the feminine third-person plural pronoun, and it is used to refer to a group of women or girls. For example, *Ellas son periodistas* ("They are journalists").

With that, Paula's explanation about Spanish subject personal pronouns came to an end. But before moving on, she added one more thing:

"Geoge, you might have noticed that we haven't mentioned the English pronoun "it." That's because there's no equivalent for "it" in

Spanish. And there's a very important reason for this: every Spanish noun is gendered, so there's no need for a neuter pronoun. All nouns in Spanish are either masculine or feminine, so we always use *él* ("he") or *ella* ("she") to refer to them, even to talk about animals, objects, and feelings! We'll talk a bit more about this later on your trip.

And the last thing you should know about pronouns for now: Verbs change to agree with subject pronouns. These changes make up the verbal paradigm of a language. Spanish is broader than English. Thanks to this, you can almost always guess who the subject of a sentence is *just from the verb*. And, since the subject can be guessed, many times, it's omitted. This is called "dropping the pronoun," and it's what most Spanish speakers do. In fact, many times, if you state the pronoun, you may be adding another layer of meaning, like emphasis or contrast."

After Paula finished talking, I felt so filled with Spanish knowledge I couldn't hold my excitement. It was a bit much, but my confidence level about the language was soaring.

When we were a couple of blocks from my hotel, Paula forgot she had to run some urgent errands, so I told her I could come with her and keep her company (the flight hadn't been so tiresome, and I wanted to keep learning some more). So, we kept driving for a while. To continue the Spanish lesson, Paula explained how I had to use the verb "to be." This was a bit more difficult:

Verb *Ser*

To explain this very important verb, Paula went back to the examples from the previous section:
- *Yo soy María* ("I am María").
- *Tú eres buena* ("You are good").
- *Usted es la jefa* ("You are the boss").
- *Él es Martín* ("He is Martín").
- *Ella es Clara* ("She is Clara").
- *Nosotras somos mujeres* ("We are women").
- *Nosotros somos chicos* ("We are boys").
- *Ustedes son mexicanos* ("You guys are Mexican").
- *Ellos son muchos* ("They are many").
- *Ellas son periodistas* ("They are journalists").

As you might have noticed, they all use the verb "to be" in English. In Spanish, all the examples have the verb *ser*. However, I didn't see the words "be" or ser in any examples. That's because the verbs are conjugated in the present tense to agree with the subject. This means that the verb takes different forms depending on who is doing the action. This happens in both languages. However, Spanish verbs change way more than English ones do.

Before showing me the ways in which the verb *ser* is conjugated in Spanish, Paula wanted to tell me something. The English verb "to be" can be translated into the Spanish verb *ser* and the Spanish verb *estar*. These two verbs have different meanings and uses. *Ser* is used for permanent states, so we use it to say WHO we are: *Yo soy María* ("I am María"). However, for temporary conditions, we use *estar*. That is why we use it to say HOW we are: *Yo estoy bien* ("I am okay"). She said she would tell me more about *estar* in the coming days.

Now it's time to see the chart she made with all the conjugations of the verb *ser* (meaning "to be" for permanent states):

	Verb "to be"	***Verbo ser***
1st person singular	I am	*Yo* **soy**
2nd person singular	You are	*Tú* **eres**
		Usted **es**
3rd person singular	He is	*Él* **es**
	She is	*Ella* **es**
1st person plural	We are	*Nosotros* **somos**
		Nosotras **somos**
2nd person plural	You are	*Ustedes* **son**

3rd person plural	They are	*Ellos* **son**
		Ellas **son**

    In the chart, we can see that some of the verbs were repeated. That means that some of the pronouns are conjugated in the same way. In total, we have ten pronouns and five conjugations.

    The pronoun *yo*, first-person singular, goes with the verbal form *soy*.

    The second-person singular pronoun *tú* takes the verbal form *eres*.

    The pronouns *usted*, *él*, and *ella*, second-person formal and third-person singular, go with the verbal form *es*.

    Since verbs don't reflect gender, *nosotros* and *nosotras*, second-person plural, go with *somos*.

    And lastly, *ustedes*, *ellos*, and *ellas*, second-person and third-person plural, take the *son* conjugation.

Introductions

We were still driving through the city, and even though I was focusing on the Spanish lesson, I couldn't keep my eyes off the buildings surrounding us. Everything was so new and colorful, so full of life. Once I learned the personal pronouns in Spanish and how to conjugate the verb *ser* in the present, Paula thought it was an excellent time to teach me how to introduce myself and others. This is what she taught me:

Simple Introductions

To say hello and introduce yourself, you can say.

- *Hola, yo soy Pedro* ("Hello, I am Pedro").

Some possible answers would be:

- *Mucho gusto, Pedro. Yo soy Sofía* ("Nice to meet you, Pedro. I am Sofía").
- *Encantada de conocerte. Yo soy Lila* ("Pleased to meet you. I am Lila").

To introduce yourself and someone else, you can say:

- *Nosotros somos Esteban y Lucas* ("We are Esteban and Lucas").
- *Nosotras somos las vecinas* ("We are the neighbors").

If you want to introduce someone else, you can say:
- *Él es Carlos* ("He is Carlos").
- *Ella es Elena* ("She is Elena").
- *Ellas son Susana y Matilde* ("They are Susana and Matilde").
- *Ellos son Martín y Alicia Gómez* ("They are Martín and Alicia Gómez").

Paula used the last sentence to discuss the "generic masculine" or **masculino genérico** in Spanish (also known as the male-as-norm principle). The concept designates the capacity of the masculine grammatical gender to name a group of both men and women. In the example above, we have a man, Martín, and a woman, Alicia. We use the masculine third-person plural pronoun *ellos* to designate both of them.

Moving on with introductions, you might also want to ask who someone is. In this case, you can say:
- *Yo soy Pablo, ¿quién eres tú?* ("I am Pablo, who are you?").
- *Yo soy Sara, ¿y usted quién es?* ("I am Sara, and who are you?").

Note that in the first example, the informal pronoun *tú* was used, and in the second example, the formal pronoun *usted* was used. There's a difference in familiarity in both sentences.

Other Introductions

Paula said that another way of introducing ourselves is by saying, "My name is." This translates to *mi nombre es* in Spanish. Let's check an example:
- *Mi nombre es Flor* ("My name is Flor")

You can also use this formula to introduce other people:
- *Su nombre es Carola* ("Her name is Carola")
- *Su nombre es Juan* ("His name is Juan")

After seeing these examples, I was struck by the fact that Spanish uses the possessive pronoun *su* both for men and women, while English uses "her" or "his," depending on the person's gender. Paula said she would explain possessive pronouns a little later.

Finally, this is how you can ask someone's name using this formula:
- *¿Cuál es tu nombre?* ("What is your name?").

- *¿Cuál es su nombre?* ("What is his/her/your name?").

One last way to introduce ourselves and others (and to ask someone's name) is to use the verb *llamarse*. This verb is a bit more complex, but don't worry, for now, Paula said I just needed to learn these ways of using it:
- *Yo me llamo Felipe* ("I am called Felipe")
- *Ella se llama Ana* ("She is called Ana")
- *¿Cómo se llama usted?* ("What are you called?")
- *¿Cómo te llamas tú?* ("What are you called?")

After her explanation, everything became much clearer, but all I could think of was how to use other Spanish verbs to carry on a conversation. I was just so eager to talk to people! When I expressed my concerns to my friend, he/she told me not to worry: she mentioned that the regular verbs in the present simple tense were a piece of cake. This is what I learned from her after we finished her errands and started heading back to my hotel:

Regular Verbs in the Present

Besides being the easiest verb tense, the Spanish *presente del indicativo* is very similar to the English present simple. That's why Paula started with it. We use this tense to talk about routines, actions that are repeated, and permanent situations.

The conjugations of the verb *ser* ("to be") that we saw earlier were *in the present*, so we already know a bit about this tense and about how Spanish verbs work. To sum it up, verbs need to agree in person and number with the person (or thing) doing the action of the verb, that is - the subject. The possible subjects we have are the pronouns we've learned: *yo, tú, usted, él, ella, nosotros, nosotras, ustedes, ellos,* and *ellas*.

So, verbs conjugated in the first-person singular *yo* ("I") behave in a particular way. Verbs conjugated in the third-person plural *ellos* and *ellas* ("they") behave differently. Verbs conjugated in the informal second-person singular *tú* ("you") behave in their own way, etc.

Luckily for me, not all verbs change as much as *ser*. *Ser* is an irregular verb, but most Spanish verbs are regular, and regular verbs follow regular patterns.

Let's delve a bit more into this. All Spanish verbs in the infinitive have one of the following endings: AR, ER, or IR. These endings are called "conjugations." The first conjugation is made up of verbs ending in AR. The second conjugation is made up of verbs ending in ER. And - you guessed it - the third conjugation is made up of verbs ending in IR.

And why is this relevant? Well, because the regular verbs of a given conjugation undergo the same changes when we conjugate them. This will become clearer when we see it in practice, so let's get down to it. We'll use three model verbs, one for each conjugation, and we'll show you how they change when we conjugate them in the present tense with each of the pronouns we know.

	am**ar** ("to love")	tem**er** ("to fear")	part**ir** ("to leave")
yo	am**o**	tem**o**	part**o**
tú	am**as**	tem**es**	part**es**
usted	am**a**	tem**e**	part**e**
él/ella	am**a**	tem**e**	part**e**
nosotros/nosotras	am**amos**	tem**emos**	part**imos**
ustedes	am**an**	tem**en**	part**en**
ellos/ellas	am**an**	tem**en**	part**en**

The truth is, the first time I saw this chart, I didn't understand a thing. But thanks to Paula's explanation, now I can explain it to you.

The good thing about the conjugation of regular verbs is that, as you can see in the chart, the first part of the verb doesn't change. We call that part "the root." To get the root of a verb, we take its infinitive and remove the AR, ER, or IR ending. To *conjugate* a verb, we keep that root and add a different ending. The ending we'll add will depend on which conjugation the verb belongs to (first, second, or third) and on the person who is doing the action, i.e., the subject.

Here are some more regular verbs conjugated for you to learn:

	buscar ("to search")	*beber* ("to drink")	*vivir* ("to live")
yo	*busco*	*bebo*	*vivo*
tú	*buscas*	*bebes*	*vives*
usted	*busca*	*bebe*	*vive*
él/ella	*busca*	*bebe*	*vive*
nosotros/nosotras	*buscamos*	*bebemos*	*vivimos*
ustedes	*buscan*	*beben*	*viven*
ellos/ellas	*buscan*	*beben*	*viven*

Just when Paula finished her explanation, we arrived at my hotel. It was a lovely building, and the door had a small sign on the right that said:

I told Paula that it meant "Welcome" and I was right! She was so proud of me. She told me she would pick me up the following day so I could visit her place. When I entered, I met the receptionist and I told her *Hola, ¿cómo está?* I wasn't able to keep talking in Spanish after that, but my effort made a big impression on her, I could tell.

Chapter Summary

Monday was a long day and I was ready to go to bed. But before I did, I wanted to review everything I had learned, so I took out a notebook and made a summary of my first day of Spanish:

- The most common ways to say hello are:
  - hola, buenos días, buenas tardes, and buenas noches.
- The most common ways to ask how someone is are:
  - *¿cómo está?*, which is more formal, and *¿cómo estás?*
- The most common ways to say goodbye are:
  - adiós, chau, and nos vemos
- The Spanish personal pronouns used in Mexico are:
  - *yo, tú, usted, él, ella, nosotros, nosotras, ustedes, ellos, ellas*
- These are the conjugations of the verb ser in the present:
  - *yo soy*
  - *tú eres*
  - *usted es*
  - *él/ella es*
  - *nosotros/nosotras somos*
  - *ustedes son*
  - *ellos/ellas son*
- We can use the verb ser to introduce ourselves and other people:
  - *Hola, yo soy Pedro.*
  - *Nosotros somos Esteban y Lucas.*
  - *Ella es Elena.*
  - *Ellos son Martín y Alicia Gómez.*
- The "generic masculine" designates the capacity of the masculine grammatical gender to name a group of both men and women.
- The presente del indicativo tense is used to talk about routines, actions that are repeated, and permanent situations.

- Spanish verbs are divided into three conjugations, depending on their ending (AR, ER, and IR), and the regular verbs of each conjugation undergo the same changes when we conjugate them.

Cultural Annex

Paula wanted to joke around, so she told me about the word **güero**. In Mexico, if you are *güero* or *güera*, that means you are blond and have fair skin.

Güero is used for men, and güera is used for women. So *güero* would be my nickname throughout the trip, which I thought was funny, to be honest.

Exercises

1. Match the following questions with their answers.
    a. *¿Cuál es tu nombre?*   1. *Bien, ¿y tú?*
    b. *Yo soy Mara, ¿quién eres tú?*   2. *Mi nombre es Sara.*
    c. *¿Cómo estás?*   3. *Yo soy Luis.*

2. Decide whether the following statement is true or false. If it's false, correct it.

    The "generic masculine" designates the capacity of the masculine grammatical gender to name a group of men.

3. Fill in the blanks of the dialogue below with one of these words: *tú, gracias, gusto, hola, estás, soy, yo*:

    Person 1: ____, yo ____ Alejandro. ¿Quién eres ____?

    Person 2: Mucho ____, Alejandro. ____ soy Nelly. ¿Cómo ____?

    Person 1: Muy bien, ____.

4. What's the difference between the pronouns *usted* and *tú*? Choose the correct answer:
    a. *Tú* is not used in Mexico, and *usted* is used in Mexico.
    b. *Tú* is informal, and *usted* is formal.
    c. *Tú* is formal, and *usted* is informal.
    d. *Tú* is a feminine pronoun, and *usted* is a masculine pronoun.

5. Decide whether the following statement is true or false. If it's false, correct it.

All regular verbs undergo the same changes when we conjugate them in Spanish.

Martes: Home Sweet Home

Tuesday morning, I woke up to the sunshine coming through the half-closed blind (I had left it that way on purpose so I would wake up as soon as the sun came up, and I did). It was a beautiful day, and I couldn't wait to meet Paula and visit her house. I went downstairs to have my continental breakfast and waited for her to arrive. When she did, I greeted her with *Hola, ¿cómo estás?* and a kiss on the cheek, like locals do.

"*¡Hola, Georgie!* You're learning so much already, and it's only been one day," she told me with a smile.

Parts of the House

We got in the car and drove a couple of miles up to her place. It was a lovely yellow house with a front yard. I was about to head up the steps when Paula stopped me. She wanted to tell me some useful Spanish words to talk about a house:

- *La casa* ("the house").
- *El edificio* ("the building").
- *El apartamento* ("the apartment").
- *La puerta* ("the door").
- *Las ventanas* ("the windows").
- *El balcón* ("the balcony").
- *Las paredes* ("the walls").

- *El techo* ("the roof").
- *El cielo raso* ("the ceiling").
- *El piso* ("the floor").
- *Las escaleras* ("the staircase").
- *La cerca* ("the fence").

Luckily, I had come prepared with my notebook, so I was able to write down every word she had said. Then, we came inside the house and stepped into the living room or, as Paula told me later, **la sala.**

"Mi casa es tu casa," Paula said, opening her arms.

I had already heard that phrase back home: it means "My home is your home" in English, but we sometimes leave it in Spanish when we talk to others.

"But what happens when you don't live in a *casa*, but in an apartment?" I asked. "Wouldn't it be *Mi apartamento es tu apartamento?*"

Paula laughed and told me it was just a figure of speech; that phrase applied to all homes, no matter their size. To my surprise, she had prepared her house for my arrival: there was a small post-it note on every piece of furniture and object on the house with its Spanish name written on it. I thanked her for this kind gesture and started reading the names of the things she had on her *sala*:

- *El sillón* ("the armchair").
- *El sofá* ("the couch").
- *El cojín* ("the cushion").
- *La mesa de centro* ("the coffee table").
- *El florero* "the vase").
- *La alfombra* ("the rug").
- *La lámpara* ("the lamp").
- *Las cortinas* ("the curtains").

Then, we went to the kitchen, or **la cocina**, so she could give me a glass of water. These were the names of the objects that were in there:

- *El horno* ("the oven").
- *El refrigerador* ("the fridge").
- *El fuego* ("the stove burner." *Fuego* also means "fire").

- *El fregadero* ("the kitchen sink").
- *El microondas* ("the microwave").
- *El tostador* ("the toaster").
- *La cafetera* ("the coffee maker").
- *El jabón lavatrastes* ("dish soap").

"Don't you have a dishwasher?" I asked with curiosity, given that I cannot live without one.

"It's not a common appliance here," replied Paula. "It's a really big purchase, and it's not that necessary to be honest. Also, it's such a waste of water and electricity, don't you think?"

She then told me a dishwasher is called *el lavavajillas*.

After the glass of water, I realized I needed to go to the toilet, so Paula showed me where the bathroom, or **el cuarto de baño**, was.

"You can also call it *el baño*, for short," said Paula before giving me privacy.

These are the Spanish post-its I found in the *baño*:
- *El inodoro* ("the toilet").
- *La ducha* ("the shower").
- *La bañadera* ("the bathtub").
- *El lavabo* ("the bathroom sink").
- *El grifo* ("the faucet").
- *El jabón para manos* ("the hand soap").
- *El cepillo de dientes* ("the toothbrush").
- *La pasta de dientes* ("the toothpaste").
- *El espejo* ("the mirror").
- *El papel higiénico* ("the toilet paper").
- *La toalla* ("the towel").

When I stepped out of the bathroom, Paula continued with her tour of the house. The next stop was the dining room, or **el comedor**. There were only three post-its here:
- *La mesa* ("the table").
- *La silla* ("the chair").
- *El mantel* ("the tablecloth").

Then, we went to the last stop of the tour: her bedroom, or **el dormitorio**.

"I haven't made my bed yet," she told me before entering the room.

"I won't judge!," I replied.

These are the words I learned inside that bedroom:
- *La cama* ("the bed").
- *Las sábanas* ("the sheets").
- *La toalla* ("the towel").
- *La colcha* ("the quilt").
- *La almohada* ("the pillow").
- *La mesa de noche* ("the nightstand").
- *El despertador* ("the alarm clock").
- *La cómoda* ("the chest of drawers").

Now that the tour was over, Paula told me it was time to learn about two very important verbs: *estar* and *haber*.

Verbs *Estar* and *Haber*

Paula started off her lesson by telling me that *estar* and *haber* mean "to be" and "to have."

"But wasn't *ser* the translation of 'to be'?" I asked with confusion.

"Yes, but in Spanish, they have different functions," replied Paula. "Remember what I told you yesterday?"

After I refreshed my memory, I realized she was right: *ser* is used for permanent states, and *estar* is for temporary conditions. That's why we ask someone *¿Cómo estás?* instead of *¿Cómo eres?* when we want to know how they are at that precise moment. However, Paula added that *estar* is also used to express location. For instance, if I wanted to say that the oven is in the kitchen, I would use the following phrase: *El refrigerador **está** en la cocina*. The word *en* is a preposition that means "in," but I learned that topic a bit later on during that same trip to Mexico.

Before giving me the complete conjugation of *estar* in the present simple tense, Paula told me that this verb is not regular, but it doesn't change that much in comparison to its bare form like *ser* does. We can still see a common root after the AR ending drops, but the endings

differed from the ones Paula had taught me the day before:
- *Yo estoy* ("I am").
- *Tú estás* ("you are," when you are addressing someone informally).
- *Usted está* ("you are," when you are addressing someone formally).
- *Él está* ("he is").
- *Ella está* ("she is," because verbs don't change according to the subject's gender).
- *Nosotros estamos* ("we are," with a masculine subject).
- *Nosotras estamos* ("we are," with a feminine subject).
- *Ustedes están* ("you are," in the plural form).
- *Ellos están* ("they are," with a masculine subject).
- *Ellas están* ("they are," with a feminine subject).

After I understood the verb *estar*, it was explained to me that the verb *haber* is used to express existence, among other uses. It can be translated as "there is" or "there are." Something interesting about the verb *haber* is that, in the present simple tense, it can only be used in its third-person singular form: *hay*. We use this word as it is, without a subject and without modifying it. This is because these types of sentences with *hay* are impersonal, since they don't reflect either the number or the person.

- *En la sala,* **hay** *un sillón* ("in the living room, there is one armchair").
- *En la sala,* **hay** *dos sillones* ("in the living room, there are two armchairs").

Paula told me that she would teach me the numbers in Spanish on the next day we met up.

Gender

As Paula told me on the first day, words in the Spanish language have their own intrinsic gender, that is, masculine or feminine (there aren't neutral words). I was shocked because this is so different from English. Types of words like nouns, pronouns, and articles follow this rule, but not verbs, which are not affected by the gender variable (You can say *Él es* and *Ella es,* and the verb will stay the same). This is clear to me when Paula was talking about people... but what about objects?

To my surprise, objects have their own gender too. She told me some rules that would help me identify a noun's gender: **if they end in -O, they tend to be masculine, and if they end in -A, that would indicate that the noun is feminine**. For example, because *casa* ends in -A, it's feminine, and *horno* is masculine because it ends in -O, so we would place the corresponding article before each world: *la casa* and *el horno*. However, rules are usually broken: there is *el dilema* ("the dilemma"), which ends in -A, but it's a masculine word.

In time, after the trip to Mexico, I got so used to Spanish gender rules that I eventually forgot about them and started to follow them by heart. It was a process, but I got there in the end.

Number

After telling me about the gender of words, Paula said it was time to talk about numbers. She had said this word before, so I knew she wasn't talking about the numbers one, two, three, etc. In grammar, number is a characteristic of nouns, pronouns, articles, adjectives, and verbs that indicate singularity or plurality. In Spanish and English, numbers work in a similar way, so it's quite easy to learn them. The only difference is that in Spanish, adjectives and articles also express numbers.

Paula showed me how words change in number using the vocabulary I had just learned. *Puerta* means "door." To talk about more than one "door," we have to add an S at the end and make it "door**s**." The same is true for the Spanish word *puerta*: the plural is *puertas*. This is true for all Spanish words ending in a vowel. For words ending in consonants, we have to add two letters: ES. So, for example, *mantel* ("tablecloth") becomes *manteles* in the plural.

All the examples Paula gave me were with nouns, but she reminded me that, in Spanish, adjectives also express numbers, so they have to change to agree with the noun they are modifying.

Adjectives

So, unlike English, there are two variables that can affect Spanish adjectives: gender and number. Luckily for us, gender follows the same rule I mentioned about the A and the O: if an adjective ends in -A, it's feminine, and if it ends in -O, it's masculine, like *viejo, vieja* (which means "old"). And numbers follow the same rule about adding an S or ES to make a singular adjective plural.

Adjectives need to be in agreement with the noun they are modifying. For instance, if I wanted to modify *casa*, which is a feminine word in its singular form, I would need an adjective in its feminine singular form, like *casa vieja* ("old house"). In English, gender and number aren't expressed by the adjective but by the noun: the sentence *casas viejas* would be "old houses," not "old**s** houses." Here are some other adjectives Paula taught me to describe objects in their four possible forms:

	Singular masculine	Singular feminine	Plural masculine	Plural feminine
Small	*Pequeño*	*Pequeña*	*Pequeños*	*Pequeñas*
Old	*Viejo*	*Vieja*	*Viejos*	*Viejas*
New	*Nuevo*	*Nueva*	*Nuevos*	*Nuevas*
Colorful	*Colorido*	*Colorida*	*Coloridos*	*Coloridas*
Modern	*Moderno*	*Moderna*	*Modernos*	*Modernas*

Paula also recommended I keep an eye on adjectives that didn't change according to the noun's gender, but only according to its number, like these ones:

	Singular masculine/feminine	Plural masculine/feminine
Big	*Grande*	*Grandes*
Soft	*Suave*	*Suaves*
Bright	*Brillante*	*Brillantes*

In this case, we would say *la casa grande* or *las casas grandes* if we were talking about more than one house. The adjective is ALWAYS determined by the noun it stands next to.

There are also some adjectives that are invariable regarding numbers; that is, they stay the same whether the noun they are modifying is plural or singular. There are not a lot of them, but *gratis* ("free") is one of them. We say *el refresco gratis* ("the free soda") and *los refrescos gratis* ("the free sodas").

Also, if I wanted to use two adjectives to modify a person, Paula said I would need to use the linking word *y*, which means "and" in Spanish. She gave me this example:

- *El apartamento es grande y moderno* ("The apartment is big and modern").

Definite Articles

Definite articles are those short words I kept hearing from Paula whenever she mentioned a noun. As in English, articles go before the noun, and they help us recognize a word's gender: for example, if we read *La ventana*, we recognize *ventana* is a singular feminine word thanks to the feminine singular article *la*. This is what Paula defines as gender and number agreement.

The definite articles' function is to tell us the noun we are talking about is a specific one. We are not talking about any window, but a particular one, so we need to use a definite article. When we say that, the person who we are talking to will know we are talking about THAT window and not another one. Paula told me that we would see indefinite articles later on.

After explaining this, she asked me to make a table with the different definite articles the Spanish language has so that I would remember. Whereas English has only one definite article ("the"), Spanish has 4!

	Masculine	Feminine
Singular	*El*	*La*
Plural	*Los*	*Las*

Colors

Then, it was time to learn about something a bit more fun: the colors! These are the names Paula told me:

- *Azul* ("blue").
- *Rojo* ("red").
- *Amarillo* ("yellow").
- *Verde* ("green").
- *Naranja* ("orange").
- *Morado* ("purple").
- *Rosa* ("pink").
- *Negro* ("black").
- *Blanco* ("white").
- *Marrón* ("brown").

These are the names of the colors, and they are nouns. Because the noun **color** ("color") is a masculine word, the colors should be masculine nouns too, so we need to place the article *el*:

- *El azul es mi color favorito* ("Blue is my favorite color").

However, sometimes we use colors to describe objects. In this case, colors would function as adjectives and, as such, should be in agreement with the noun's gender and number. As we said before, there are some adjectives that only change according to the noun's number, like the following ones:

- *El sillón azul, los sillones azules* ("The blue armchair, the blue armchairs").
- *La toalla verde, las toallas verdes* ("The green towel, the green towels").
- *El cojín naranja, los cojines naranjas* ("The orange cushion, the orange cushions").
- *La colcha rosa, las colchas rosas* ("The pink quilt, the pink quilts").
- *La silla marrón, las sillas marrones* ("The brown chair, the brown chairs").

Then, there are colors that, as adjectives, need to be in agreement with the noun's number *and* gender:
- *Los almohadones rojos, las mesas rojas* ("The red cushions, the red tables").
- *Los despertadores amarillos, las cortinas amarillas* ("The yellow alarm clocks, the yellow curtains").
- *Los cepillos de dientes morados, las sábanas moradas* ("The purple toothbrushes, the purple sheets").
- *Los hornos negros, las ventanas negras* ("the black ovens, the black windows").
- *los pisos blancos, las paredes blancas* ("the white floors, the white walls").

These are some examples I could come up with when describing Paula's house:
- *El sofá es rojo* ("The couch is red").
- *Las cortinas son blancas* ("The curtains are white").

I use the verb *ser* instead of *estar* because we're talking about a defining quality of the object.

Chapter Summary

After a second day of sightseeing and learning Mexican Spanish, I sat down at the desk in my hotel room and made a summary of everything I had learned.
- First, I learned the names of the parts of the house, such as: *la sala, el cuarto de baño, el comedor* and *la cocina.*
- I also learned the names of furniture and appliances, like: *el sillón, la mesa, el inodoro* and *el lavavajillas.*
- Then, Paula taught me all about two important verbs:
  - *Estar,* which is used for temporary conditions and to express location.
  - *Haber,* which is used to express existence.
- Then, we talked about gender, numbers, and adjectives. I learned that Spanish adjectives change to agree in gender and number with the noun they are modifying.
- After adjectives, we moved to the four definite articles: *el, la,*

- *los,* and *las.*
- To finish today's lesson, Paula chose a brighter subject: the colors!

Cultural Annex

Before I went to bed, Paula sent me a text with a famous Mexican saying. This is what her message said:

"I almost forgot! **Anda como Juan por su casa** is a saying that means 'To be a man in his own house' in English. It's used to talk about the trust someone has towards a place or person that isn't close to them. For example, if you knocked on a stranger's door in your hotel, went inside, and used their shower, this person might say *Este señor anda como Juan por su casa.* Got it? *¡Hasta mañana!*"

The example Paula gave me was funny, so I laughed and wished her good night.

Exercises

1. Transform the following adjectives into their feminine, plural versions:
   a. *Moderno*
   b. *Viejo*
   c. *Morado*
   d. *Negro*
   e. *Pequeño*
2. Decide whether the following statement is true or false. If it's false, correct it:
   In Spanish, adjectives usually go before the noun they are modifying, as in English.
3. Classify the following Spanish word according to the part of the house they belong in, and then determine whether they are masculine or feminine:
   a. *Mesa*
   b. *Alfombra*
   c. *Toalla*
   d. *Fuego*
   b. *Espejo*

4. Translate the following sentences from English to Spanish:
   a. "The table is old"
   b. "There is an old green chair"
   c. "The fridge is in the kitchen"
5. Find the correct sentence out of the three given options:
   a. The verbs *estar* and *ser* mean different things in English.
   b. In the present simple tense, the verb *haber* can be used only in the third-person singular form.
   c. All adjectives have a masculine and feminine version.

Miércoles: Family Tree

On Wednesday, Paula had a surprise for me. It was her niece's birthday, so her family was getting together to celebrate it. And she invited me to join them! On our way there, she told me a bit more about Mexican families.

In Mexico, and also in Mexican families living abroad, people take care of their elders. Many times, grandparents live in the same house with their children and grandchildren. And not only grandparents! A kid might live with their siblings, parents, grandparents, cousins, aunts, and uncles. Growing up, Paula lived with ten people!

Paula told me that for her and for most people in Mexico, the family unit is made up of parents and siblings, but also extended family. She is close to her grandparents, godparents, aunts, uncles, cousins, nieces, nephews, and second cousins.

Family bonds are strong: people help the members of their family when they are sick or in trouble. Besides, Mexican families gather to celebrate many dates: birthdays, national holidays, graduations, and important Catholic days like baptisms, the first communion, and weddings. Many times, these gatherings take place at some family member's homes, and they can involve up to fifty people!

The Family

Paula took me to her brother's house to celebrate her niece's second birthday. It was a lovely celebration! There was plenty of homemade food, a beautiful cake, and a piñata. Besides, there were a lot of people.

Some were friends, but most of them were relatives. I had my notebook with me, so, as Paule introduced me to her family in English and Spanish, I wrote everything down:

Close Family

Paula started introducing me to her close family, that is, *su familia cercana*, and this is what I wrote down:

- *La madre* ("the mother").
- *La mamá* ("the mom").
- *El padre* ("the father").
- *El papá* ("the dad").
- *La esposa* ("the wife").
- *El esposo* ("the husband").
- *El hijo* ("the son").
- *La hija* ("the daughter").
- *Los hijos* ("the children").
- *Los hermanos* ("the siblings").
- *El hermano/la hermana mayor* ("the older brother/sister").
- *El hermano/la hermana menor* ("the younger brother/sister").
- *El hermano/la hermana del medio* ("the middle brother/sister").
- *Los mellizos/las mellizas* ("the non-identical twins")
- *Los gemelos/las gemelas* ("the identical twins")

Paula said that, in Mexico, non-identical twins are sometimes called **cuates** in a loving way. The word *cuate* is also used to refer to a friend. For example, you can say *Tú eres mi cuate*, which means "You are my mate."

Extended Family

Then we moved on to the rest of the family:

- *El abuelo* ("the grandfather").
- *La abuela* ("the grandmother").
- *Los abuelos* ("the grandparents").
- *El nieto* ("the grandson").
- *La nieta* ("the granddaughter").
- *Los nietos* ("the grandchildren").

- *El tío* ("the uncle").
- *La tía* ("the aunt").
- *El primo* ("the male cousin").
- *La prima* ("the female cousin").
- *El sobrino* ("the nephew").
- *La sobrina* ("the niece").
- *La familia política* ("the in-laws").
- *El cuñado* ("the brother-in-law").
- *La cuñada* ("the sister-in-law").
- *El suegro* ("the father-in-law").
- *La suegra* ("the mother-in-law").
- *La nuera* ("the daughter-in-law").
- *El yerno* ("the son-in-law").
- *El padrastro* ("the stepfather").
- *La madrastra* ("the stepmother").
- *La hermanastra* ("the stepbrother").
- *El hermanastro* ("the stepsister").
- *El medio hermano* ("the half-brother").
- *La media hermana* ("the half-sister").
- *El hijastro* ("the stepson").
- *La hijastra* ("the stepdaughter").
- *El padrino* ("the godfather").
- *La madrina* ("the godmother").
- *El ahijado* ("the godson").
- *La ahijada* ("the goddaughter").
- *Los parientes lejanos* ("the distant relatives").
- *El primo/tío tercero* ("the third cousin/uncle").
- *La tía/prima segunda* ("the second cousin/aunt").
- *El pariente lejano* ("the distant relative").

Types of Families

Then she told me how to name the different types of families:

- *La familia tradicional* ("the traditional family").

- *La familia ensamblada* ("the blended family").
- *El matrimonio del mismo sexo* ("the same-sex marriage").
- *El matrimonio de dos mujeres* ("the same-sex marriage of two women").
- *El matrimonio de dos hombres* ("the same-sex marriage of two men").
- *La familia homoparental* ("the rainbow family").
- *La familia monoparental* ("the single parent family").

Possessive Pronouns and Adjectives

I loved meeting Paula's family. They were all super nice to me: they spoke slowly so that I could understand them, and they answered all the questions I had. Also, I had some great Mexican homemade food!

After I had been having fun for a while, Paula took me to the kitchen table, and we sat down. She wanted to talk to me a bit about Spanish grammar, specifically about *possessives.*

To talk about her family members, Paula had been using the word *mi* before the noun, as we do in English with the word "my": *Ella es* **mi** *mamá* translates to "She is **my** mom." Both *mi* an "my" are possessives. We use them to clarify whose mother, son, aunt, father, etc. we are talking about. In other words, possessives are used to talk about possession, ownership, and belonging.

One curious thing about Spanish possessives is that they have to agree in gender and number with the noun that is possessed, not with the possessor. Don't worry; at first, I didn't understand it either, but it became clearer with some examples.

In both English and Spanish, we have two types of possessives. For example, "my" and "mine" translate to *mi* and *mío/mía*. The first are called possessive adjectives, and the second possessive pronouns. Luckily for us, Paula took the time to explain them in more detail.

Possessive Adjectives

Possessive adjectives go before the noun and show that a person or thing belongs to another. Since they are adjectives, they behave like any other Spanish adjective: they agree in number (and sometimes in gender) with the thing that they are modifying, that is, the person or object that is possessed. To make things clearer, Paula showed me this chart with all the possessive adjectives:

Possessor	The thing that is possessed	
	Singular	Plural
yo	mi	mis
tú	tu	tus
usted	su	sus
él/ella	su	sus
nosotros/nosotras	nuestro (if the thing is masculine) nuestra (if the thing is feminine)	nuestros (if the things are masculine) nuestras (if the things are feminine)
ustedes	su	sus
ellos/ellas	su	sus

Since this chart can be a bit difficult to go through, Paula also provided with a lot of examples, and she used her family to make it fun!

- *Ella es **mi** mamá* ("She is **my** mom").
- *Él es **mi** papá* ("He is **my** dad").
- *Ellos son **mis** padres* ("They are **my** parents").

Here, we can see how *mis* agrees in the plural with *padres*, the people "possessed," not with the possessor, *yo*.

- *Yo soy **tu** amiga* ("I am **your** friend").
- *¿Dónde viven **tus** hermanas?* ("Where do **your** sisters live?").

The same happens in this example: the possessive adjective *tus* agrees in the plural with *hermanas*.

- *Disculpe, señor, ¿su esposa está aquí?* ("Excuse me, sir, is **your** wife here?").
- *Esos son **sus** asientos* ("Those are **your** seats").

And one more time: in English, we say "your wife" and "your seats." In these cases, "your" is invariable, but in Spanish, we say *su esposa*, in the singular, and *sus asientos*, in the plural.

- *Él es **mi** hermano Martín, y ella es **su** hija Ema* ("This is **my** brother Martín, and she is **his** daughter Ema").
- *Mi prima es **su** amiga* ("My cousin is **her** friend").
- *Ema está contenta porque están **sus** amigos* ("Ema is happy because **her** friends are here").

Here, we can see some more differences between both languages. In Spanish, when the owner is he or she, that is, the third-person singular, the possessive adjective is *su* for singular nouns (*su hija, su amiga*) and *sus* for plural nouns (*sus amigos*). It doesn't matter if the owner is masculine or feminine.

- *Niños, ¿dónde están **sus** primos?* ("Kids, where are **your** cousins?").
- ***Nuestras** primas están por aquí y **nuestros** primos por allí* ("**Our** female cousins are over here and **our** male cousins are over there").

Nuestro, nuestros, nuestra and *nuestras* all mean "our." These possessive adjectives have to agree in number **and gender** with the thing or person that's possessed: we say *nuestras primas* ("our female cousins") in the feminine plural and *nuestros primos* ("our male cousins") in the masculine plural.

- *Lisa es **su** hermana, por lo tanto Beto y Paco son **sus** sobrinos* ("Lisa is **their** sister, so Beto and Paco are **their** nephews").

And here, one last time. In *su hermana* ("their sister"), *su* goes in the singular, even though the "possessor" is "they" because it agrees with *hermana*. On the other hand, in *sus sobrinos* ("their nephews"), *sus* goes in the plural.

Possessive Pronouns

After talking about possessive adjectives, Paula moved on to possessive pronouns. Like all pronouns, possessives take the place of a noun. We use them instead of nouns in the sentence. To determine which possessive pronoun we need, Paula told me I had to pay attention to the gender and number of the thing possessed and to the person and number of the possessor. As always, to make it clearer, she showed me a chart with all the possessive pronouns:

Possessor	The thing that is possessed			
	Singular		Plural	
	Feminine	Masculine	Feminine	Masculine
yo	*mía*	*mío*	*mías*	*míos*
tú	*tuya*	*tuyo*	*tuyas*	*tuyos*
usted	*suya*	*suyo*	*suyas*	*suyos*
él/ella	*suya*	*suyo*	*suyas*	*suyos*
nosotros/nosotras	*nuestra*	*nuestro*	*nuestras*	*nuestros*
ustedes	*suya*	*suyo*	*suyas*	*suyos*
ellos/ellas	*suya*	*suyo*	*suyas*	*suyos*

And let's check some examples:
- *Ese coche es* **mío** ("That car is **mine**").
- *Ellas no son mis primas. Las* **mías** *están acá* ("These are not my cousins. **Mine** are over here").
- *¿Tienes tu llave? La* **mía** *está rota* ("Do you have your key? **Mine** is broken").
- *¿Me prestas tu goma? Perdí las* **mías** ("Can I borrow your eraser? I lost **mine**").

As we can see, when I am the owner, in English, we use "mine." In Spanish, we have four translations for "mine": *mío* is used for masculine singular nouns; *mía* is used for feminine singular nouns; *míos* is used for masculine plural nouns; and *mías* is used for feminine plural nouns.

- *¿Ese vaso es **tuyo**?* ("Is that glass **yours**?").
- *Esos no son tus zapatos. Los **tuyos** están allá* ("Those are not your shoes. **Yours** are over there").
- *Podemos usar mi llave. La **tuya** está rota, ¿no?* ("We can use my key. **Yours** is broken, right?").
- *Usas mi goma porque siempre pierdes las **tuyas*** ("You use my eraser because you always lose **yours**").

When the possessor is someone we refer to as *tú*, the possessive pronoun in English is "yours." In Spanish, we also have four options: *tuyo* for masculine singular nouns, *tuya* for feminine singular nouns, *tuyos* for masculine plural nouns, and *tuyas* for feminine plural nouns.

- *Esa casa es **nuestra*** ("That house is **ours**").
- *¿De quién es ese coche? El **nuestro** está en casa* ("Whose car is that? **Ours** is at home").
- *¿Dónde trabajan tus padres? Los **nuestros** son médicos* ("Where do your parents work? **Ours** are doctors").
- *¿Puedes traer dos cucharas? Las **nuestras** están rotas* ("Can you bring two spoons? **Ours** are broken").

When we are the possessors or owners, the possessive pronoun in English is "ours." In Spanish, we use *nuestro* for singular masculine nouns, *nuestra* for singular feminine nouns, *nuestros* for plural masculine nouns, and *nuestras* for plural feminine nouns.

- *Señora, ¿ese abrigo es **suyo**?* ("Madam, is that coat **yours**?").
- *Esas no son sus compras, señor. Las **suyas** están allá* ("Those are not your groceries, sir. **Yours** are over there").
- *Podemos usar mi bote. El **suyo** está roto* ("We can use my boat. **Hers** is broken").
- *¿Esas son tus sandalias? No, esas son las **suyas*** ("Are those your sandals? No, those are **his**").
- *Esos son mis parientes. ¿Los **suyos** dónde están?* ("Those are my relatives. Where are **yours**?").
- *Mi paquete es este. ¿Y el **suyo**?* ("My package is this. What about **theirs**?").

When the thing possessed belongs to someone we refer to as *usted*, or to a third-person or group of people, in Spanish, we use *suyo* for masculine singular nouns, *suya* for feminine singular nouns, *suyos* for masculine plural nouns, and *suyas* for feminine plural nouns.

However, since this can be a bit confusing (*suyo, suya, suyos, suyas* are used for a number of people), sometimes it is better to use the preposition *de* plus the subject personal pronoun, like in the following examples:

- *Señora, ¿ese abrigo es* **de usted***?* ("Madam, is that coat **yours**?").
- *Esas no son sus compras, señor. Las* **de usted** *están allá* ("Those are not your groceries, sir. **Yours** are over there").
- *Podemos usar mi bote. El* **de ella** *está roto* ("We can use my boat. **Hers** is broken").
- *¿Esas son tus sandalias? No, esas son las* **de él** ("Are those your sandals? No, those are **his**").
- *Esos son mis parientes. ¿Los* **de ustedes** *dónde están?* ("Those are my relatives. Where are **yours**?").
- *Mi paquete es este. ¿Y el* **de ellos***?* ("My package is this. What about **theirs**?").

Numbers from 0 to 100

After a lovely afternoon with Paula's family, it was time to go back to my hotel. My friend offered me a lift, and I was thankful because I was quite tired. However, as it had become customary on this trip, she made the most of the journey and started asking me questions to teach me some more Spanish:

"Georgie," she said, "tell me a bit about your family. Do you have any brothers or sisters? How old are your parents? How many cousins do you have?"

I started telling her about my family, but she stopped me and asked me to do it in Spanish. I tried, but I still hadn't learned the numbers! So, she set out to explain to me how numbers work in Spanish.

From 0 to 9

There's not much logic in numbers from 0 to 9, so Paula said the best thing is to learn them by heart:

- 0: *Cero*
- 1: *Uno*
- 2: *Dos*
- 3: *Tres*
- 4: *Cuatro*
- 5: *Cinco*
- 6: *Seis*
- 7: *Siete*
- 8: *Ocho*
- 9: *Nueve*

From 10 to 19

From 10 to 19, some words start repeating, but again, these numbers should be learned by heart.

- 10: *Diez*
- 11: *Once*
- 12: *Doce*
- 13: *Trece*
- 14: *Catorce*
- 15: *Quince*
- 16: *Dieciséis*
- 17: *Diecisiete*
- 18: *Dieciocho*
- 19: *Diecinueve*

From 20 to 29

Now, things start having some logic. From *veintiuno* ("twenty-one") to *veintinueve* ("twenty-nine"), numbers are one word made up of the suffix *veinti-* plus the numbers from *uno* to *nueve*.

- 20: *Veinte*
- 21: *Veintiuno*
- 22: *Veintidós*
- 23: *Veintitrés*

- 24: *Veinticuatro*
- 25: *Veinticinco*
- 26: *Veintiséis*
- 27: *Veintisiete*
- 28: *Veintiocho*
- 29: *Veintinueve*

From 30 to 39

When we reached the thirties, Paula asked me to pay special attention because this is the logic that numbers follow from *treinta y uno* ("thirty-one") to *noventa y nueve* ("ninety-nine"): first we have the tens (*treinta, cuarenta, cincuenta, sesenta, setenta, ochenta, noventa*), then the conjunction *y* ("and") and finally the numbers from *uno* to *nueve*. Let's check it out:

- 30: *Treinta*
- 31: *Treinta y uno*
- 32: *Treinta y dos*
- 33: *Treinta y tres*
- 34: *Treinta y cuatro*
- 35: *Treinta y cinco*
- 36: *Treinta y seis*
- 37: *Treinta y siete*
- 38: *Treinta y ocho*
- 39: *Treinta y nueve*

From 40 to 100

- 40: *Cuarenta*
- 50: *Cincuenta*
- 60: *Sesenta*
- 70: *Setenta*
- 80: *Ochenta*
- 90: *Noventa*
- 100: *Cien*

After learning the numbers from *cero* to *cien*, I still wasn't able to answer Paula's questions about my family! I still didn't know how to say the verb "to have," and I also didn't know how to talk about age. Luckily for me, Mexico City has one of the world's worst traffic, so the journey back to my hotel stretched on, and Paula taught me some more Spanish.

Verb *Tener*

The Spanish verb *tener* means "to have." As it happens with a lot of words, it has some other meanings, like "to hold." But Paula said that, for now, we would be focusing on the "to have" meaning.

This is how the verb *tener* is conjugated in the present for all the pronouns we know:

- *Yo tengo* ("I have").
- *Tú tienes* ("you have").
- *Usted tiene* ("you have").
- *Él tiene* ("he has").
- *Ella tiene* ("she has").
- *Nosotros tenemos* ("we have").
- *Nosotras tenemos* ("we have").
- *Ustedes tienen* ("you have").
- *Ellos tienen* ("they have").
- *Ellas tienen* ("they have").

Apart from giving the conjugation, Paula said some sentences out loud, and I wrote them down in my notebook:

- *Yo tengo cuatro hermanas y dos hermanos* ("I have four sisters and two brothers").
- *Nosotras tenemos muchos primos y primas* ("We have a lot of cousins").
- *Yo tengo dos trabajos* ("I have two jobs").
- *Él no tiene trabajo* ("He doesn't have a job").
- *¿Tú tienes trabajo?* ("Do you have a job?").
- *¿Cuántos hermanos tiene usted?* ("How many siblings do you have?").

- *¿Cuántos años tienes?* ("How old are you?").
- *¿Cuántos años tienen tus padres?* ("How old are your parents?").
- *Yo tengo treinta y seis años* ("I am thirty six years old").

These last three examples puzzled me. To have years? What did Paula mean by that? When I asked her, she said:

"The thing is, Georgie, in Spanish, to talk about age, we don't use the verbs *ser* or *estar*, the equivalents to the verb 'to be.' Instead, we use the verb *tener*. So, if I translated literally the question *¿Cuántos años tienes?* It would be 'How many years do you have'? It's quite simple."

After learning about numbers and the verb *tener*, I was able to tell Paula a bit about my family. This is what I said:

- *Yo tengo tres hermanos: dos hermanas y un hermano* ("I have three siblings: two sisters and one brother").
- *Mi hermana mayor tiene cuarenta y un años* ("My elder sister is forty one years old").
- *Mi hermana menor tiene treinta años* ("Mi younger sister is thirty years old").
- *Mi hermano tiene treinta y cuatro años* ("My brother is thirty four years old").
- *Mi mamá tiene setenta años. Mi papá tiene sesenta y ocho años* ("My mom is seventy years old. My dad is sixty eight years old").
- *Yo tengo nueve primos* ("I have nine cousins").

Short Story about The Family

After Paula finished with her explanation, she proceeded to tell me about her family in Spanish:

Mi **familia** tiene <u>cuarenta y dos</u> integrantes. Yo tengo <u>cuatro</u> **hermanas** y <u>dos</u> **hermanos**. Yo soy la **hermana del medio**: Carlos y Martín son mis **hermanos menores** y son **gemelos**. Ellos tienen <u>veintinueve</u> años. Ellos son mis **medios hermanos**: son **hijos** de mi **papá** y su nueva **esposa**, Carmela. Mis **hermanas mayores** se llaman Gimena, Manuela, Laura y Patricia. Patricia tiene <u>treinta y dos</u> años, yo tengo <u>treinta y seis</u>, Laura tiene <u>treinta y siete</u>, Manuela tiene <u>treinta y nueve</u> y Gimena tiene <u>cuarenta y uno</u>. Nuestro papá se llama Alberto y nuestra **mamá** se llama

*Cristina. Ambos tienen la misma edad: <u>sesenta y cinco</u> años. Sus padres y madres (es decir, mis **abuelos** y **abuelas**) no están vivos, pero se llamaban Tomás, Juan Pablo, María Rosa y Esther. Tengo muchos **sobrinos** y **sobrinas**. Por ejemplo, Ema, la **hija** de Martín, tiene <u>dos</u> años. Yo soy su **tía**. Mi **esposo** se llama Esteban y tenemos un **hijo**. Él se llama Vicente y <u>tiene</u> diez años.* Todos los años celebramos Navidad en familia.

This is the translation Paula helped me make:

"My **family** has <u>forty-two</u> members. I have <u>four</u> **sisters** and <u>two</u> **brothers**. I am the **middle sister**: Carlos and Martín are my **younger brothers,** and they are **identical twins**. They are <u>twenty-nine</u> years old. They are my **half-brothers**: they are the **children** of my dad and his new **wife**, Carmela. My **older sisters** are called Gimena, Manuela, Laura and Patricia. Patricia is <u>thirty-two</u>, I am <u>thirty-six</u>, Laura is <u>thirty-seven</u>, Manuela is <u>thirty-nine</u> and Gimena is <u>forty-one</u>. Our **father's** name is Alberto and our **mother's** name is Cristina. They are both the same age: <u>sixty-five</u>. Their **fathers** and **mothers** (that is, my **grandfathers** and **grandmothers**) are not alive, but their names were Tomás, Juan Pablo, María Rosa and Esther. I have many **nieces** and **nephews**. For example, Martin's **daughter** Ema is <u>two</u> years old. I am her **aunt**. My **husband's** name is Esteban and we have a **son**. His name is Vicente and he is <u>ten</u> years old. Every year we celebrate Christmas together."

Chapter Summary

Wednesday, that is, *miércoles*, was a fun but exhausting day. When I finally got to my hotel, I had a bath, ordered a glass of wine, and sat down to review all the things I had learned:

- First, Paula told me all about the Mexican family. She also taught me a lot of vocabulary about:
    - The close family, like la mamá, el papá, el hermano and la hermana.
    - The extended family, like los primos, los tíos, los padrinos and los ahijados.
    - Types of family, like la familia tradicional and la familia ensamblada.

- Then, Paula told me about possessives.
    - I learned the possessive adjectives: mi, mis, tu, tus, su, sus, nuestro, nuestros, nuestra, nuestras.
    - I also learned about possessive pronouns such as mía, mías, mío, míos, suya, suyas, suyo and suyos.
- Then it was time for numbers: Paula taught me the numbers in Spanish from *cero* to *cien*.
- Finally, I learned about the verb *tener*, which means "to have," and it is used to talk about age.

Cultural Annex

During the birthday party, I heard the word *padre* a lot – which I had learned means "father." At one point, I asked Paula whose father everyone was talking about, and she burst out laughing. I thought I had misunderstood what everyone was saying, but when she stopped laughing, Paula gave an explanation.

Besides meaning "father," *padre* is used informally as an adjective equivalent to "cool," "good," "great," or "big." Mexicans also use *padrísimo*, the superlative of *padre*. So it's common to hear expressions like:

- *¡Qué día tan padre!* ("It's such a nice day!").
- *Tu casa está padrísima* ("Your house is wonderful").
- *Esta fiesta de cumpleaños está muy padre* ("This birthday party is awesome").

Paradoxically, the word *madre* ("mother") is also used colloquially in Mexican Spanish, but, in this case, with a negative connotation. The full expression is *valer madre*, and it means not to care about something:

- *Me vale madre* ("I don't care").
- *Está lloviendo, pero nos vale madre* ("It's raining, but we don't care").

When Paula explained this expression to me, she told me to be careful because it could be considered rude.

Exercises

1. How do you say eighty-four in Spanish?

   a. *Ochenticuatro*

   b. *Ochocientos cuatro*

   c. *Ocho cuatro*

   d. *Ochenta y cuatro*

2. Match the following Spanish words with their English translation.

   a. *Primo segundo*   1. Single-parent family

   b. *Familia monoparental*   2. Son in law

   c. *Yerno*   3. Second cousin

3. Decide whether the following statement is true or false. If it's false, correct it.

   In Spanish, possessive pronouns agree in gender and number with the person who possesses the object in question.

4. Are the following sentences grammatically correct? Correct the wrong ones:

   a. *Ella es mía prima.*

   b. *Yo tiene ocho hermanos.*

   c. *¿Él es suyo abuelo?*

5. Answer the following questions in Spanish with complete answers following the example:

   Example: *¿Qué edad tienes? Yo tengo ... años.*

   a. *¿Cuántos hermanos y hermanas tienes?*

   b. *¿Qué edad tiene tu madre?*

   c. *¿Cuántos tíos y tías tienes?*

Jueves: Food for Days

After a long day of sightseeing in Mexico City, Paula texted me and invited me to dinner. I had been waiting for this moment since the day I arrived in Mexico. I'm quite a foodie, so I was quite excited to taste some local dishes.

It was 5 p.m., and Paula hadn't come to the hotel to pick me up yet. I was worried something had happened to her, so I sent her a text to check. She replied the following:

"It's FIVE in the afternoon, Georgie! In México, we eat a little later than that. Does 8 o'clock work for you? You can have a *merienda* at the hotel."

"A *merienda*?" I thought with confusion when I read her message. She told me that *merienda* is the meal that comes after lunch and before dinner because people in Mexico go to bed later than people in the U.S. I meant to complain, but I had to accept it. If I am in another country, I have to follow its customs, even if that meant having a snack in the hotel.

When the sun set and the evening began, Paula arrived and took me with her car to a lovely place in Ccoyoacán, the city's historical center. We went to a lovely restaurant called *Belinda*, which specialized in traditional Mexican food.

General Vocabulary

When we arrived, I was instantly struck by the aroma of fire and spices. *Belinda* was a family restaurant and it was packed with locals eager to have their daily dose of Mexico. Despite being so crowded, we were able to find a spot because Paula had already booked a table for two. We sat at a booth near the window and before we looked at the menu, my friend saw an opportunity to teach me more Spanish vocabulary:

- *La comida* ("the food")
- *La bebida* ("the drink")
- *El desayuno* ("the breakfast")
- *El almuerzo* ("the lunch")
- *La merienda* ("the afternoon snack," a meal served between 4 and 6 p.m.)
- *La cena* ("the dinner," between 7 and 9 p.m.)
- *El menú* ("the menu")
- *El platillo* ("the dish")
- *La entrada* or *el entrante* ("the starter")
- *El platillo principal* ("the main course")
- *El postre* ("the dessert")
- *Los cubiertos* ("the cutlery")
- *El tenedor* ("the fork")
- *El cuchillo* ("the knife")
- *La cuchara* ("the spoon")
- *El vaso* ("the glass")
- *La servilleta* ("the napkin")

Food and Drinks

When I opened the menu and started skimming through it, I faced a huge problem: everything was in Spanish! Paula laughed at me for expecting a different scenario, but helped me translate some of the words:

- *El elote* ("the corn")
- *La cebolla* ("the onion")
- *El chile* ("the chili")
- *Los frijoles* ("the beans")
- *Las habas* ("fava beans")
- *El nopal* (an edible cactus)

- *El aguacate* ("the avocado")
- *El queso* ("the cheese")
- *El jitomate* ("the tomato")
- *La lechuga* ("the lettuce")
- *La ternera* ("the beef")
- *El pollo* ("the chicken")
- *El pescado* ("the fish")
- *El cerdo* ("the pork")
- *El agua* ("the water")
- *El vino* ("the wine")
- *La cerveza* ("the beer") or *la chela*, as Mexicans like to call it
- *El jugo* ("the juice")
- *El café* ("the coffee")
- *El chocolate* ("the chocolate," just like in English)
- *La manzana* ("the apple")
- *La naranja* ("the orange," like the color)

Verbs Related to Food, Cooking and Eating

Because I couldn't decide what dish I wanted, Paula suggested we order some Mexican classics for me to try. While we waited for our dinner to arrive, my friend taught me some verbs I could use when talking about food:

- *Comer* ("to eat")
- *Beber* or *tomar* ("to drink")
- *Probar* ("to taste")
- *Desayunar* ("to have breakfast")
- *Almorzar* ("to have lunch")
- *Merendar* ("to have an afternoon snack")
- *Cenar* ("to have dinner / to dine")
- *Cocinar* ("to cook")
- *Cortar* ("to cut")
- *Hornear* ("to bake")
- *Hervir* ("to boil")
- *Freír* ("to fry")

Mexican Dishes

Finally, the food arrived! All the dishes looked amazing and were an explosion of flavor. These were the delicious local dishes Paula had ordered:

- **Los tacos.** I'd already tried tacos back home, but those were nothing compared to the ones I had at this restaurant. The hand-sized corn tortillas were so soft and flavorful! Paula ordered many different types of tacos:
  - *al pastor*: these tacos have grilled beef, which is made in a similar way to kebab meat, and they also have *piña* ("pineapple" in Spanish).
  - *de Birria* (my favorite): they have braised mutton, which is marinated with *chiles, jitomate*, and some spices.
  - *de nopal: nopal* is an edible cactus, and it's mixed with cheese.
  - *de carnitas:* they have *cerdo* and *cebollas*.
  - *gobernador:* they have *camarones* ("shrimps" in Spanish) and peppers.
  - *quesadillas:* they only have *queso*!
- **El guacamole.** I also knew this dish (a dip made of *aguacate, cebolla,* and sometimes *jitomate),* but the one I had at this restaurant was so light and refreshing.
- **Las enchiladas.** This dish was a bit spicier than I could handle, but it was still delicious. *Enchiladas* also have corn tortillas, but they are covered in a spicy sauce and meat.
- **Los burritos.** I wasn't sure what the difference between *burritos* and *tacos* was. Paula told me that the *tortillas* used in *burritos* are bigger, are made of wheat flour, and are rolled around different fillings. These *burritos* had a filling made of *carne* and *frijoles*.
- **Los tamales.** This dish consisted of a package of corn leaves with a *maíz* filling. Paula nagged me when I tried to eat the leaves! She said that only the filling is edible and that other variations of this dish can be found throughout Latin America.
- **El mole.** I was surprised to see this stew. This one was packed with ingredients like *pollo*, spices, nuts, and lots of *chiles*. Paula

told me there are about fifty types of *mole* in Mexico!

Key Phrases at A Restaurant

Not a trace of sauce was left when we finished eating. Our bellies were full, and so were our hearts. Even though my body had suffered from the food's heat, I absolutely enjoyed every bite I had. While we were waiting for the check, I started to write down some of the phrases Paula used at the *restaurante*:

- Tengo una reserva para dos personas a nombre de Solís ("I have a reservation for two under Solís")
- ¿Cuál es el menú del día? ("What's today's special?")
- ¿Este platillo tiene nueces? Soy alérgica a los frutos secos ("Does this dish have walnuts? I'm allergic to nuts")
- Estamos listos para pedir ("We're ready to order")
- Me gustarían las enchiladas de ternera, por favor ("I'd like the beef enchiladas, please")
- ¿Me pasarías la sal, por favor? ("Could you pass me the salt, please?")
- La cuenta, por favor ("The check, please")
- ¿Puedo envolver esto para llevar? ("Can I wrap this up to go, please?")

These are not my original notes, of course (I didn't have the necessary listening skills to catch all the phrases yet). Paula helped me by correcting my spelling and grammar mistakes.

After paying and leaving a generous *propina* ("tip" in Spanish), we drove around the city. The streets were filled with people and life, and it was a beautiful experience. Because it was past my bedtime, I felt a little sleepy, so Paula dropped me off at my hotel and called it a night. Going to bed with a full stomach had never felt so good! The next day would be a new day filled with new adventures.

Chapter Summary

In order not to forget all I'd learned on that day, I stayed up a little bit more just to revise:

- First of all, I learned some general vocabulary about food, like *el almuerzo* or *los cubiertos*.

- Second of all, I saw some interesting vocabulary about food and drinks, like *la cebolla* and *el pollo*.
- Then, I focused on verbs we use to talk about food, like *comer* and *cocinar*.
- After that, I learned the names of some of the delicious Mexican *platillos* we ate.
- Finally, I wrote down some key phrases to use inside a restaurant, like *La cuenta, por favor*.

Cultural Annex

After we ate, Paula thought it would be a good idea to teach me some local sayings:

- *A darle que es mole de olla* ("Let's do it fast, there's no time").
- *Ponerle mucha crema a los tacos* ("Being too dramatic").
- *De chile, mole y pozole* ("Of all varieties").

Exercises

1. How do you say these words in Spanish? And what about their corresponding verbs?

   a. Breakfast / To have breakfast

   b. Lunch / To have lunch

   c. Afternoon snack / To have an afternoon snack

   d. Dinner / To have dinner

2. For each of the following three categories, write three examples that correspond:

a. Vegetables

b. Cutlery

c. Meats

3. Decide whether the following statement is true or false. If it's false, correct it.

   In Spanish, in order to ask for the check, you can say the following: *El cheque, por favor*.

4. Are the following sentences correct? Correct the wrong ones:
   a. Tengo un reserva para dos personas a nombre de Gutiérrez.
   b. ¿Cuál es el menú especial?
   c. ¿Puedo volver esto para llevar?
   d. *Somos listos para pedir.*
5. What phrase do you use to talk about someone who is being too dramatic?

Viernes: Around The City

Four days into my Mexican adventure, everything was going great: I had eaten the most delicious meals, and I had met Paula's family, an opportunity that allowed me to practice my Spanish with natives. I couldn't be luckier. However, I felt that I wasn't taking advantage of being in a foreign city. There was so much to discover and so many places to visit! Luckily for me, Paula had it all planned out: she was going to take me on a tour around Mexico City!

When Paula told me she was downstairs, I was so excited I forgot the keys to my hotel room. I just couldn't wait to see the city. It was going to be a lovely day.

Tourist Attractions

We visited a lot of places throughout the city. Paula told me the Spanish names of the usual landmarks in a city:

- *El museo* ("the museum")
- *El teatro* ("the theater")
- *El cine* ("the cinema")
- *El estadio* ("the stadium")
- *La plaza central* ("the central square")
- *El parque* ("the park")
- *La catedral* ("the cathedral")
- *La iglesia* ("the church")

- *La estatua* ("the statue")
- *La fuente* ("the fountain")
- *El ayuntamiento* ("the city hall")
- *La avenida principal* ("the main avenue")
- *El puerto* ("the port")

Verb *Ir*

Paula told me that if I wanted to walk around the city, there was one verb I should know without a doubt: the verb *ir*. This verb means "to go" and, just like *ser*, is a really special irregular verb, one that changes its root significantly compared to its bare form:

- Yo voy
- Tú vas
- Usted va
- Él va
- Ella va
- Nosotros vamos
- Nosotras vamos
- Ustedes van
- Ellos van
- Ellas van

"As you can see, Georgie," said Paula, "the endings also differ a bit from the ones I've taught you in the past. *Yo voy* has a similar ending to the verb *ser*, which is *soy*. However, the first-person plural has the typical MOS ending."

Directions

Paula thought it would be a good idea to visit a History museum called *el Museo de la Ciudad de México*. As she wasn't so sure how to get there from where we were standing at the time, she started asking for directions. These are some of the phrases that can be used to do that:

- *Disculpe / Perdone* ("Excuse me," because it's always nice to be polite)
- *¿Dónde está el museo?* ("Where is the museum?")

- *¿Cómo llego al museo?* ("How do I get to the museum?")
- *¿Podría decirme cómo llegar al museo, por favor?* ("Could you tell me how to get to the museum, please?")
- *¿En qué calle está el museo?* ("What street is the museum on?")
- *¿El museo está cerca?* / *¿El museo está lejos?* ("Is the museum nearby?" / "Is the museum far?")

This is when I learned the verb *llegar*, which means "to arrive" or "to get."

Indefinite Articles

Once she found out how to get to the museum, she taught me how to ask for directions if I wasn't looking for any museum in particular. She told me that I had to learn about indefinite articles, I wrote them in bold within the phrases she used as an example:

- *¿Hay **algún** museo cerca?* ("Is there **a** museum nearby?")
- *¿Sabe si hay **un** cine por aquí?* ("Do you know if there's **a** cinema around?")

Indefinite articles are used to talk about unknown or generic nouns. In English, I use three articles of this kind: "a," "an," and "some." However, in Spanish, there are four basic types. This is a table Paula sketched in my notebook:

	Masculine	Feminine
Singular	*Un*	*Una*
Plural	*Unos*	*Unas*

"But what about the word *algún*?" I asked Paula.

"*Algún* means 'any,'" replied Paula. "They tend to be used interchangeably. *Algún* is a masculine singular word, but there are also three other variants of gender and number."

After saying this, she proceeded to write another small table:

	Masculine	Feminine
Singular	*Algún*	*Alguna*
Plural	*Algunos*	*Algunas*

Verbs of Movement

On the way to the museum, Paula thought it would be a good idea to teach me some verbs of movement in addition to *ir*:

- *Venir* ("to come")
- *Llegar* ("to arrive" or "to get")
- *Viajar* ("to travel")
- *Volver* ("to return")
- *Entrar* ("to enter")
- *Salir* ("to go out")
- *Subir* ("to go up")
- *Bajar* ("to go down")
- *Caminar* ("to walk")
- *Conducir* ("to drive")

Prepositions and Adverbs of Place

Once Paula finished explaining, she moved on to the prepositions of place and movement. I've written them down within an example phrase so as to also practice verbs of movement:

- **en** ("in," "at," or "inside"). *Yo estoy **en** la playa* ("I am at the beach")
- **entre** ("between"). *El museo está **entre** el parque y el teatro* ("The museum is between the park and the theater")
- **bajo** ("under"). *Yo camino **bajo** un puente* ("I walk under a bridge")
- **sobre** ("on" or "on top of"). *Yo camino **sobre** la avenida principal* ("I walk on the main avenue")

- ***desde*** ("from"). *Yo viajo **desde** los Estados Unidos* ("I travel from the United States")
- ***hasta*** ("to" or "as far as"). *Ellos caminan **hasta** la iglesia* ("They walk to the church")
- ***hacia*** ("toward"). *Ellos conducen **hacia** Veracruz* ("They drive toward Veracruz")
- ***por*** ("by" or "through"). *Yo paso **por** la catedral* ("I walk by the cathedral")

Then, Paula taught me some adverbs (that is, a type of word that characterizes a verb) in Spanish to talk about place and movement:

- ***encima*** ("on top of"). *Estoy **encima** del edificio* ("I'm on top of the building")
- ***dentro*** ("inside"). *Estoy **dentro** del cine* ("I'm inside the cinema")
- ***fuera*** ("outside"). *María está **fuera** del estadio* ("María is outside the stadium")
- ***delante*** or ***enfrente*** ("in front of"). *Estoy **delante** del ayuntamiento* ("I am in front of the city hall")
- ***frente a*** ("opposite"). *Carlos **está** frente al hotel* ("Carlos is opposite the hotel")
- ***detrás*** ("behind"). *La plaza principal está **detrás** del museo* ("The main square is behind the museum")
- ***al lado de*** o ***junto a*** ("next to"). *El cine está **junto al** estadio* ("The cinema is next to the stadium")
- ***cerca*** ("close to"). *Están **cerca** de la plaza* ("You are close to the square")
- ***lejos*** ("far"). *La iglesia está **lejos** de la avenida principal* ("The church is far from the main avenue")
- ***debajo*** ("under")
- ***alrededor*** ("around")
- ***aquí*** ("here")
- ***allí*** ("there")

After I wrote down the examples, I noticed that there were two prepositions that Paula hadn't mentioned during her explanation: ***del*** and ***al***. When I asked her what those were, she told me they were called *contracciones*, or "contractions" in English. This happens when we use the prepositions **de** and **a** followed by the masculine singular article **el**. The blend of the two vowel sounds makes it easier to pronounce for speakers. These are the only *contracciones* in the Spanish language.

Short Story about The City

We finally arrived at the *Museo de la Ciudad de México,* which was three blocks away from the *Zócalo,* the main square of Mexico City. This eighteenth-century building stood tall and showcased brick walls that stayed strong during the passage of time. When we entered, Paula grabbed a couple of leaflets about the history of Mexico City and handed me one. This is what it said:

En el año 1325, antes de los españoles, la ciudad antigua **estaba** <u>sobre</u> *un valle y* **había** *montañas* <u>alrededor</u> *de las casas. Los aztecas* **vivían** <u>en</u> *Tenochtitlán. Ese* **era** *el antiguo nombre de la Ciudad de México. Durante el 1500, el español Hernán Cortés y sus hombres* **caminaban** <u>por</u> *la ciudad. Tenochtitlán* **cambiaba** *mucho año a año. Por ejemplo, los españoles* **construían** *edificios nuevos* <u>junto a</u> *los viejos. Los nativos no* **eran** *libres:* **dependían** *de los reyes de España. En 1821, los mexicanos* **pedían** *la independencia. Hoy, la ciudad tiene mucha vida e historia,* <u>desde</u> *sus catedrales* <u>hasta</u> *sus mercados*

Paula helped me translate, and we highlighted some prepositions and adverbs of place:

"In the year 1325, before the Spaniards, the ancient city **was** <u>on top of</u> a valley, and **there were** mountains <u>around</u> the houses. The Aztecs **lived** <u>in</u> Tenochtitlan. That **was** the ancient name of Mexico City. During the 1500s, the Spaniard Hernán Cortés and his men **walked** <u>through</u> the city. Tenochtitlán **changed** a lot from year to year. For example, the Spaniards **built** new buildings <u>next to</u> the old ones. The natives **were** not free: they **were dependent** on the kings of Spain. In 1821, the Mexicans **demanded** independence. Today, the city has a lot of life and history, <u>from</u> its cathedrals <u>to</u> its markets."

The museum was really interesting, and I really learned an extraordinary amount of things.

The Past Tense (*pretérito imperfecto*)

When I finished reading the leaflet, something strange caught my attention.

"Those verbs do not have the endings we learned before, right?." I asked Paula.

"Indeed," she replied. "They are talking about past events, so they are in a type of past tense which is called *pretérito imperfecto,*"

According to Paula, we use the *pretérito imperfecto* (literally translated as "the imperfect past tense") when we want to talk about actions, events, or processes that started and finished in the past. This tense, like the rest of the tenses, has to agree with the person and number of the subject. We use this tense when we want to talk about actions, situations, or events which took place in the past, but with no temporal limits. We use it to talk about how our life used to be and the things we used to do, that is, habits of the past. We also use it to talk about ongoing actions in the past that were interrupted. Finally, *pretérito imperfecto* is used to describe past feelings, characteristics, and conditions. It can be translated to the past simple, but it can be used with the expression "used to."

"There is also a *pretérito perfecto* (or 'perfect past tense' if you will), but we'll talk about it another time, don't worry! I don't want to burn you out; you are on vacation, after all."

She reminded me that we classify Spanish verbs into three groups according to their endings. Verbs ending in AR belong to the first conjugation or *la primera conjugación*. Verbs ending in ER belong to *la segunda conjugación*. And verbs ending in IR are part of *la tercera conjugación*. We do this because regular verbs of each conjugation follow the same pattern when we conjugate them in a verb tense.

Paula taught me the first conjugation of the verb *entrar*, which means "to enter":

- *Yo entraba*
- *Tú entrabas*
- *Usted entraba*
- *Él entraba*
- *Ella entraba*
- *Nosotros entrábamos*

- *Nosotras entrábamos*
- *Ellos entraban*
- *Ellas entraban*

There are four pronouns that have the same conjugation: for **yo, usted, él,** and **ella**, we need to drop the AR ending and add **ABA**: *entraba*.

Then, for **tú,** we need to drop the AR ending and add **ABAS**: *entrabas*.

For **nosotros** and **nosotras**, we have to drop the AR ending and add **ÁBAMOS**, with an accent mark: *entrábamos*.

Finally, for **ellos** and **ellas**, we need to drop the AR ending and add **ABAN**: *entraban*.

Fortunately, Paula told me that the second and third conjugations followed the same rule when it comes to the *pretérito imperfecto*. She explained this to me with the verbs *volver* and *subir* ("to return" and "to go up" respectively):

- *Yo volvía*
- *Tú volvías*
- *Usted volvía*
- *Él volvía*
- *Ella volvía*
- *Nosotros volvíamos*
- *Nosotras volvíamos*
- *Ellos volvían*
- *Ellas volvían*
- *Yo subía*
- *Tú subías*
- *Usted subía*
- *Él subía*
- *Ella subía*
- *Nosotros subíamos*
- *Nosotras subíamos*
- *Ellos subían*
- *Ellas subían*

Paula told me that, for **yo, usted, él** and **ella**, we need to drop the ER/IR ending and add **ÍA**: *volvía/subía*.

Then, for **tú** we need to drop the ER/IR ending and dd **ÍAS**: *volvías/subías*.

For **nosotros** and **nosotras**, we have to drop the ER/IR ending and add **ÍAMOS**, with an accent mark: *volvíamos/subíamos*.

Finally, for **ellos** and **ellas**, we need to drop the ER/IR ending and add **ÍAN**: *volvían/subían*.

"And what about the verb *ir*?" I asked Paula. "Should I say *iría* if I wanted to use the *pretérito imperfecto*?"

"No, not quite," answered Paula. "*Yo iría* exists, but that verb is in the conditional tense, meaning 'I would go'. The root of the verb *ir* in the *pretérito imperfecto* is IB, but the endings change a bit because it is a really irregular verb."

These are the conjugations for all the personal pronouns:
- *Yo iba*
- *Tú ibas*
- *Usted iba*
- *Él iba*
- *Ella iba*
- *Nosotros íbamos*
- *Nosotras íbamos*
- *Ustedes iban*
- *Ellos iban*
- *Ellas iban*

Here are some examples Paula gave me:
- *Yo iba a la escuela todas las mañanas* ("I went to school every morning")
- *¿Tú ibas a karate con Sara cuando eras pequeño?* ("Did you go to karate with Sara when you were little?")
- *Usted, señor, iba al trabajo cada jueves* ("You, sir, went to work each Thursday")
- *Él iba a Italia cada verano* ("He went to Italy every summer")

- *Estela iba al cine los viernes.* ("Estela went to the movies on Fridays")
- *Nosotros íbamos a la plaza de niños* ("We went to the square when we were kids")
- *Nosotras íbamos a Veracruz cada año* ("We went to Veracruz each year")
- *Ustedes iban al campo los fines de semana* ("You went to the countryside on the weekends")
- *Ellos iban al teatro con su madre* ("The went to the theatre with her mother")
- *Ellas iban siempre a comer pasta* ("They always went to eat pasta")

Chapter Summary

After a long day of sightseeing, Paula dropped me off at my hotel, and she went back to her place. Because I was so excited about all that I'd learned, I decided to review everything the moment I entered my room:

- First of all, I learned useful vocabulary about city landmarks.
- Second of all, I focused on the verb *ir* and its conjugation in the present simple: *yo voy, tú vas, usted va, él/ella va, nosotros/as vamos, ustedes van* and *ellos/as van.*
- Third of all, I learned how to ask for directions and about the following indefinite articles: *un, una, unos, unas, algún, alguna, algunos* and *algunas.*
- Then, I focused on verbs, prepositions, and adverbs of movement.
- After that, I read an interesting leaflet about Mexico City's history.
- Finally, I focused on the *pretérito imperfecto* (a tense about past habits, feelings, characteristics, and conditions) and its endings for every type of conjugation:
    - ABA, ABAS, ÁBAMOS, and ABAN for the first conjugation
    - ÍA, ÍAS, ÍAMOS and ÍAN for the second and third conjugation

o For the verb *ir*, the conjugation changed a little: *yo iba, tú ibas, usted iba, él/ella iba, nosotros/as íbamos, ellos/as iban.*

Cultural Annex

In case I forgot the names of the places we visited on our tour around *Mexico City*, I wrote down all the historical landmarks we saw and the ones we didn't, but I'll definitely will when I return to the country:

- **La Plaza de la Constitución (Zócalo).** This is the historical and political heart of Mexico City and a gathering point for cultural, social, and political events.
- **La Basílica de Nuestra Señora de Guadalupe.** This is a religious and cultural sanctuary for the Mexican people. Its grand architecture and spiritual significance make it the place of pilgrimage *par excellence*.
- **El Palacio de Bellas Artes.** This architectural gem is the home of a wonderful art collection and offers a wide range of cultural shows. Its Art Nouveau and Art Deco style captivates every visitor who walks through its doors.
- **El Castillo de Chapultepec.** This former imperial residence and imperial headquarters was turned into a lovely museum. Because of its privileged location, it features fantastic panoramic views of the city.
- **La Catedral Metropolitana.** This majestic Baroque cathedral features impressive towers, and it's known for its rich history from the times of the Spanish rule, when Mexico was a colony.
- **El Templo Mayor.** These archaeological ruins reveal the greatness of the ancient Tenochtitlán and are a window into the past, the intriguing Pre-Hispanic times.
- **Xochimilco.** These meandering canals are surrounded by nature and colorful *trajineras*, a type of boat decorated with traditional Mexican symbols.
- **La Casa Azul (Museo Frida Kahlo).** Because of its cultural significance, Frida Kahlo's former home was transformed into a museum painted in blue (hence the name "The Blue House").
- **Torre Latinoamericana.** This icon of Mexico's modern architecture offers panoramic sightseeing from its spectacular

viewpoint.
- **Museo de Arte Popular.** This museum exhibits the artisanal richness of Mexico and highlights the diversity of techniques and materials used by the different regions of the country.
- **Mercado San Juan.** A gastronomical paradise with authentic Mexican flavors. It offers a wide range of fresh and exotic products to taste and enjoy.
- **Estadio Azteca.** If you are a soccer fan, this historic *fútbol* stadium witnessed legendary moments from the history of the sport.

Exercises

1. Name the eight indefinite articles mentioned in this chapter.
2. Match the following words to its English translation:

    a. el ayuntamiento   i. the church
    b. la avenida principal   ii. the main avenue
    c. la iglesia   iii. the city hall
    d. la fuente   iv. the fountain

3. Write the whole conjugation for the verb *ir*, both in the present simple tense and in the *pretérito imperfecto*.
4. Are the following sentences to ask for directions correct? Correct the wrong ones:

    a. ¿Qué llego al cine?
    b. ¿El parque está lejos?
    c. ¿Podría decirme cómo ir al museo, gracias?

5. Decide whether the following statement is true or false. If it's false, correct it.

    In the *pretérito imperfecto*, these are the endings that correspond to the first conjugation: ÍA, ÍAS, ÍAMOS and ÍAN.

Sábado: Field Trip

Of course, I wanted to go to Mexico to visit my friend Paula and to learn some Spanish. However, I was also hoping to go to the beach at least for one day. That's why I was a bit disappointed when Paula told me that the closest beach was 320 kilometers away, that is, 200 miles. I only had two days left in my holiday, and spending eight hours driving sounded like a waste of time, unless...

"What if we made the most of the time in the car? You could teach me vocabulary related to traveling, and I'm sure there are a few grammar topics you are dying for me to learn."

"Okay, Georgie, you win. *Nos vamos a la playa.* We are going to the beach. But we have to leave very early in the morning, so you better have everything ready when I pick you up."

"Sure, you can count on it."

"Oh, and one more thing. While you pack for the field trip, make a vocabulary list of all the items of clothing. It's not a difficult topic; I believe you can study it on your own."

What's in My Bag?

Like most people, I don't particularly enjoy waking up early, let alone on a Saturday holiday, to make a vocabulary list! But I had promised Paula to be ready at 6 a.m. and to learn clothing vocabulary on my own. Therefore, I had a coffee while looking up words in the dictionary.

I started with the items I use to carry other things:
- *El equipaje* ("the luggage").
- *El equipaje de mano* ("the carry-on").
- *La maleta* ("the suitcase").
- *La mochila* ("the backpack").
- *El bolso* ("the handbag").
- *La cartera* ("the wallet").
- *El maletín* ("the briefcase").

Of course, I hadn't brought *un maletín* to my vacation, but I use one when I go to the office, so I wanted to learn the Spanish word for that.

Then I looked up items of clothing for the torso:
- *La playera* ("the t-shirt").
- *La camiseta sin mangas* ("the tank top").
- *La blusa* ("the blouse").
- *El vestido* ("the dress").
- *El suéter* ("the sweater").
- *La chamarra* ("the jacket").
- *La sudadera* ("the hoodie").
- *El abrigo* ("the overcoat").

In my suitcase, I didn't have *abrigos, suéteres* nor *chamarras*. Only a couple of *sudaderas* in case it got cooler at night.

Next, I looked up items of clothing for the lower part of the body.
- *Los vaqueros* ("the jeans").
- *Los pantalones* ("the pants").
- *Los pantalones cortos* ("the shorts").
- *La falda* ("the skirt").

I packed a pair of *pantalones cortos* for my day trip to the beach, and I continued my research on footwear.
- *El calzado* ("the footwear").
- *Los zapatos* ("the shoes").
- *Los tenis* ("the sneakers").
- *Las zapatillas* ("the high heels").
- *Las botas* ("the boots").

- *Las chancletas* ("the flip flops").
- *Las sandalias* ("the sandals").

While looking up some of these words, I found out a fun fact: In Spain, "sneakers" are called *las zapatillas,* and "high heels" are *los zapatos de tacón.* So, *zapatillas* mean two very different things in Mexico and in Spain!

I made the last section about underwear:
- *La ropa interior* ("the underwear").
- *Las bragas* ("the panties").
- *El sostén* ("the bra").
- *Los calzoncillos* ("the underpants").
- *Los calcetines* ("the socks").
- *Las medias de nylon* ("the stockings").
- *El traje de baño* ("the swimsuit").
- *El bañador* ("the swimsuit").

When I finished, I grabbed my *bañador, una gorra* ("a cap"), and a pair of *gafas de sol* ("sunglasses"), and I was ready to go!

Telling The Time

As I said before, Paula was picking me up at 6 a.m. from my hotel. As soon as I sat down in the passenger seat, she asked me:

"What time is it, George?"

"It's 6 a.m."

"And can you say that in Spanish?"

"Well, 'six' is *seis*..."

"Good, let me teach you the rest."

Paula started with some vocabulary. She taught me the following words:
- *El reloj* ("the clock, the watch").
- *La hora* ("the time, the hour").
- *El minuto* ("the minute").
- *El segundo* ("the second").
- *En punto* ("o'clock").
- *Y media* ("half past").

- *Y cuarto* ("a quarter past").
- *Menos cuarto* ("a quarter to").
- *Aproximadamente* ("approximately").
- *De la mañana* ("a.m., in the morning").
- *Mediodía* ("midday").
- *De la tarde, de la noche* ("p.m., in the afternoon, at night").

After this vocabulary, she moved on to the basic question for asking the time:

- *¿Qué hora es?* ("What time is it?").

Despite being the basic question to ask the time, unless you are talking to someone close to you, it can be a bit rude to say it just like that. These are some more polite variations to ask strangers:

- *Disculpe, ¿qué hora es?* ("Excuse me, what time is it?").
- *Disculpe, ¿puede por favor decirme la hora?* ("Excuse me, can you tell me the time, please?").
- *Perdona, ¿qué hora es?* ("Sorry, what time is it?").
- *Perdona, ¿puedes decirme la hora, por favor?* ("Sorry, can you tell me the time, please?").

If you want to ask about a specific time or schedule, these are some questions you can ask:

- *¿A qué hora es...?* ("At what time is...?").
- *¿A qué hora es el partido?* ("At what time is the match?").
- *¿A qué hora sale el tren?* ("At what time does the train leave?").
- *¿A qué hora vienes?* ("At what time are you coming?").

After that lesson, I was ready to tell the time. In order to test me, Paula asked me *¿Qué hora es?* throughout the day, and these were my answers:

- *Son las siete menos cuarto de la mañana* ("It's a quarter to seven in the morning").
- *Son las diez en punto de la mañana* ("It's ten o'clock").
- *Son las doce y media del mediodía* ("It's 12:30 p.m.").
- *Son las tres y diez de la tarde* ("It's ten past three in the afternoon").

- *Son las cinco menos veinte de la tarde* ("It's twenty to five in the afternoon").

At The Beach

A few minutes after 10 a.m., we reached our destination: Tecolutla Beach in Veracruz. Tecolutla is a nice tourist town located between the Tecolutla River and the Gulf of Mexico. We were hungry, hot, and tired from the drive, so we bought some tacos and juices and headed to the beach to rest.

After a refreshing swim in the ocean and a power nap, I was ready for some more Spanish! Paula thought it would be fun to tell me the names of all the things we saw around us! This is the list I made.

- *La tumbona* ("the deck chair").
- *La pelota de playa* ("the beach ball").
- *La sombrilla* ("the beach umbrella").
- *El bote* ("the boat").
- *La hielera* ("the cooler").
- *El guardavidas, la guardavidas* ("the lifeguard").
- *El faro* ("the lighthouse").
- *El muelle* ("the pier").
- *El velero* ("the sailboat").
- *Las olas* ("the waves").
- *La arena* ("the sand").
- *El castillo de arena* ("the sandcastle").
- *La toalla* ("the towel").
- *El pareo* ("the sarong").
- *La carpa* ("the tent").
- *El protector solar* ("the sunscreen").

Demonstratives

Learning the names of the things we saw around us was fun, but I still needed to learn something else to be able to say: "Look at that sandcastle." Paula told me that "this," "that," "these," and "those" are English demonstratives. Like possessives, demonstratives have two functions. They can work as adjectives, that is, describing a noun (as in

"Look at that sandcastle"), and they can also work as a pronoun, that is, taking the place of a noun (as in "Look at that"). We use demonstratives to point at people or things.

English demonstratives take into account two dimensions: distance from the speaker and whether the noun is singular or plural. Therefore, if something is close to us, we say "this" if it's singular and "these" if it's plural; and if something is far from us, we say "that" if it's singular and "those" if it's plural.

Spanish demonstratives also change depending on the number of the nouns and the distance from the speaker, but there are three possible distances to take into account. Besides, as always, we have to consider gender, and not only masculine and feminine, because there are neuter demonstratives. That's why Spanish has fifteen demonstratives instead of four. This is the chart Paula showed me:

Object/Person	Masculine		Feminine		Neuter
	Singular	Plural	Singular	Plural	
Close to the speaker	este	estos	esta	estas	esto
Close to the addressee	ese	esos	esa	esas	eso
Far from both	aquel	aquellos	aquella	aquellas	aquello

To clarify the chart, Paula told me that the distance refers to the distance between the object or person being pointed at and the person speaking. If the object or person is close to the speaker, we use the first row: *este, estos, esta, estas, esto.*

If the object or person mentioned is close to the addressee, we use the second row: *ese, esos, esa, esas, eso.*

Finally, if the object or person is far from everyone involved in the conversation, we use the last row: *aquel, aquellos, aquella, aquellas, aquello.*

The singular and plural columns are easy to understand. And also: the masculine and feminine ones. They refer to the gender and number of the object or person we are pointing at. However, there's a neuter column that needs some explanation. Neuter demonstratives are invariable regarding gender and number. We use them to talk about abstract ideas or situations, to make general statements, and to point at unknown nouns when we don't know which gender they are. These demonstratives are only used as pronouns, though. It sounds a bit confusing, but it will become clearer with some examples.

Demonstrative Adjectives

Paula started by giving me examples of the demonstratives used as adjectives:

- *Mira **este** castillo de arena que hice* ("Look at **this** sandcastle I made").
- *Quiero **ese** pareo* ("I want **that** sarong").
- ***Aquel** muelle es nuevo* ("**That** pier **over there** is new").
- *¿**Estas** chancletas son tuyas?* ("Are **these** flip flops yours?").
- *Trae **esas** tumbonas* ("Bring **those** deck chairs").
- ***Aquellas** carpas se alquilan* ("**Those** tents **over there** are for rent").

All in all, Spanish demonstrative adjectives aren't that different from the English ones.

Demonstrative Pronouns

Then, Paula gave me some examples of demonstrative pronouns:

- *No quiero esos tacos, prefiero **estos*** ("I don't want those tacos, I prefer **these**").
- *¿Por qué te gustan más **esos**?* ("Why do you like **those** more?").
- *¿Quiénes son **aquellos**?* ("Who are **those**?").
- ***Esta** es mi toalla* ("**This** is my towel").
- ***Esa** es la tuya* ("**That** one is yours").
- *¿Y **aquella** de quién es?* ("And whose is **that** one **over there**?").

Again, I found that, besides having to take into account the three levels of distance and the two genders, demonstratives working as pronouns were quite simple. Finally, it was time for the neuter

demonstrative pronouns:
- *¿Qué es **esto**?* ("What is **this**?").

In this example, since the speaker doesn't know what the thing is, they can't assign it a gender, so they use the neuter pronoun *esto*.
- ***Eso** es mentira* ("**That** is a lie").

In this case, the neuter pronoun *eso* is used because the speaker is referring to an abstract idea.
- ***Aquello** de lo que hablamos sucedió* ("**That thing** we talked about happened").

In this example, the speaker is also talking about an abstract idea. The difference with *eso* is that, by using *aquello*, the idea seems to be further away in time.

And with that, the lesson about demonstratives came to an end, and I was able to enjoy my beach day for a while.

Irregular Verbs in the Present

My trip to Mexico was coming to an end, and there was one thing that was troubling me. On my first day, Paula taught me how to conjugate regular verbs in the present, and I was doing well in that regard. Also, throughout the week, we saw the conjugation of some irregular verbs, such as ser, estar, haber, tener, and *ir*. I had learned them by heart, and I was using them correctly.

However, I was still afraid of irregular verbs. So, to comfort me, during the drive back to Mexico City, Paula told me about some Spanish irregular verbs that can be grouped together because they follow certain patterns. She said that there are six groups of irregular verbs.

First Group

The first group is made up of verbs that are only irregular for the first-person singular pronoun *yo*. These verbs follow the regular pattern of conjugation for all the rest of the pronouns, but in the first-person singular, they undergo some kind of change in the root. An example of this group is the verb *hacer* ("to do"), which has the following conjugation:
- *Yo hago* ("I do").
- *Tú haces* ("you do").
- *Usted hace* ("you do").

- *Él hace* ("he does").
- *Ella hace* ("she does").
- *Nosotros hacemos* ("we do").
- *Nosotras hacemos* ("we do").
- *Ustedes hacen* ("you do").
- *Ellos hacen* ("they do").
- *Ellas hacen* ("they do").

As you can see, the only irregular conjugation is the first one, where the C from the root changes to a G. In this group, we can also include the following verbs:
- *Poner, yo pongo* ("I put").
- *Traer, yo traigo* ("I bring").
- *Dar, yo doy* ("I give").
- *Valer, yo valgo* ("I am worth").
- *Saber, yo sé* ("I know").
- *Caber, yo quepo* ("I fit").
- *Oír, yo oigo* ("I hear").
- *Ver, yo veo* ("I see").
- *Caer, yo caigo* ("I fall").
- *Salir, yo salgo* ("I leave").

Paula didn't give the conjugations of these verbs for the rest of the pronouns because they follow the regular pattern!

Second Group

In the second group, we had verbs ending in a vowel + CIR/CER. Again, these verbs are only irregular when we conjugate them in the first-person. The change they undergo is the addition of a Z between the vowel and the C. Let's check some examples:
- Trad**uc**ir, yo trad**uzc**o ("I translate").
- Cond**uc**ir, yo cond**uzc**o ("I drive").
- Enalt**ec**er, yo enalt**ezc**o ("I exalt").
- Con**oc**er, yo con**ozc**o ("I know").

As for the rest of the pronouns, these verbs behave like regular verbs; we don't need those conjugations.

Third Group

The third group has verbs ending in UIR. To conjugate them with all pronouns except for *nosotros* and *nosotras*, we add a Y between the root and the ending. *Construir* ("to build") belongs to this group. Let's check its conjugation:

- *Yo construyo* ("I build").
- *Tú construyes* ("you build").
- *Usted construye* ("you build").
- *Él construye* ("he builds").
- *Ella construye* ("she builds").
- *Nosotros construimos* ("we build").
- *Nosotras construimos* ("we build").
- *Ustedes construyen* ("you build").
- *Ellos construyen* ("they build").
- *Ellas construyen* ("they build").

This group also has verbs such as *destruir* ("to destroy"), *intuir* ("to suspect"), *huir* ("to flee"), and *excluir* ("to exclude").

Fourth Group

In the fourth group, we have verbs that change an O of the root for UE, but otherwise follow the regular pattern. This is true for all pronouns except for the first-person plural *nosotros* and *nosotras*, which follow the regular pattern. *Dormir* ("to sleep") belongs to this group:

- *Yo duermo* ("I sleep").
- *Tú duermes* ("you sleep").
- *Usted duerme* ("you sleep").
- *Él duerme* ("he sleeps").
- *Ella duerme* ("she sleeps").
- *Nosotros dormimos* ("we sleep").
- *Nosotras dormimos* ("we sleep").
- *Ustedes duermen* ("you sleep").
- *Ellos duermen* ("they sleep").
- *Ellas duermen* ("they sleep").

Acostarse ("to lie down") and *probar* ("to try") also belong in this group.

Fifth Group

The fifth group is also made up of verbs with a vocalic change in the root: in this case, from an E to IE. Again, these changes apply to all pronouns except for *nosotros* and *nosotras*. In this group, we can name the verb *pensar* ("to think"):

- *Yo pienso* ("I think").
- *Tú piensas* ("you think").
- *Usted piensa* ("you think").
- *Él piensa* ("he thinks").
- *Ella piensa* ("she thinks").
- *Nosotros pensamos* ("we think").
- *Nosotras pensamos* ("we think").
- *Ustedes piensan* ("you think").
- *Ellos piensan* ("they think").
- *Ellas piensan* ("they think").

Despertar ("to wake up") and *entender* ("to understand") also belong to this group. When Paula mentioned these two verbs, I was a bit confused because both have two Es in the root. Which one should I change for IE to conjugate them? Easy, the vowel that changes is always the one that's closest to the ending. *Yo despierto, yo entiendo.*

Sixth Group

Finally, **the last group** gathers verbs with a third vocalic change. In this case, the verbs change an E in the infinitive to an I in the present. As with the previous changes, the pronouns *nosotros* and *nosotras* maintain their root. *Pedir* ("to ask for") belongs to this group:

- *Yo pido* ("I ask for").
- *Tú pides* ("you ask for").
- *Usted pide* ("you ask for").
- *Él pide* ("he asks for").
- *Ella pide* ("she asks for").
- *Nosotros pedimos* ("we ask for").
- *Nosotras pedimos* ("we ask for").
- *Ustedes piden* ("you ask for").
- *Ellos piden* ("they ask for").
- *Ellas piden* ("they ask for").

Vestir ("to dress") also belongs to this group and undergoes this change.

After this explanation, I felt a little bit better. I know the irregularities are a lot to learn and that there are still other verbs that are completely irregular and don't follow any of these patterns. However, learning to find some kind of coherence in the irregularities was really comforting to me.

Chapter Summary

After our day trip, Paula dropped me off at my hotel at 10:30 p.m. -*las diez y media de la noche*. I was so tired I almost went to bed straight away. But I didn't want to break my routine. I took a shower to wash the beach off me and sat down to review and organize my notes:

- The day had started off with me learning clothing vocabulary. I made a vocabulary list with:
    - Luggage, such as *la maleta, el bolso,* and *la mochila*.
    - Tops, like *la playera, la sudadera,* and *la camiseta sin mangas*.
    - Trousers, like *la falda, los vaqueros,* and *los pantalones cortos*.
    - Footwear, such as *los tenis, las botas,* and *las sandalias*.
    - Underwear, like *el sostén, los calcetines,* and *los calzoncillos*.
- Then, Paula taught me how to talk about the time:
    - I learned some vocabulary like *el reloj, la noche, el mediodía,* and *la hora*.
    - The way to ask the time is: *¿Qué hora es?*
    - The way to tell the time is: *Son las* + the hour + *de la mañana/de la tarde/de la noche*.
- When we arrived at the beach, I learned some beach vocabulary, such as *el faro, el muelle,* and *el velero*.
- Then it was time to learn all about the demonstratives, both adjectives and pronouns: *este, estos, esta, estas, esto, ese, esos, esa, esas, eso, aquel, aquellos, aquella, aquellas, aquello*.

- Finally, Paula calmed my fears by telling me about six types of irregularities in the present.

Cultural Annex

Even though our field trip to the beach was rather short, Paula recommended some lovely beaches in Mexico to visit on my next trip:

- **Playa del Carmen, Quintana Roo.** Located in the Riviera Maya, this beach is famous for its crystal-clear waters, white sand, and vibrant atmosphere. This is an ideal destination for diving and snorkeling.
- **Playa de Punta Morena, Cozumel, Quintana Roo.** This beach is located in a secluded area, an island away from tourist areas. Its waters with blue and green tones are a sight for sore eyes. Its natural beauty offers a relaxing experience.
- **Cabo San Lucas, Baja California Sur.** This area features stunning beaches, such as the famous *Playa del Amor* and the rock formation of *El Arco*. It offers opportunities for water sports and is known for its nightlife and luxurious resorts.
- **Puerto Escondido, Oaxaca.** Known as a surfer's paradise, this beach has some of the country's most challenging and exciting waves. It also has the beautiful *Bahía Principal* ("Main Bay"), perfect for swimming and relaxing.
- **Playa Langosta, Cancún, Quintana Roo.** This public beach offers calm and shallow waters, perfect for families with small children. There are *palapas* (places to eat and drink) and shaded areas, a perfect scenario for a carefree day in the sun.

Exercises

1. Are the words **in bold** demonstrative pronouns or demonstrative adjectives? Read each sentence and determine whether each word in bold is <u>a pronoun or an adjective</u>, and determine whether it's <u>close to the speaker, close to the addressee, or far from both</u>:
    a. ***Aquel*** *barco tiene velas blancas.*
    b. *Me gusta **esta**, no aquella.*
    c. ***Eso*** *es un gran problema para nosotros.*
    d. ***Estos*** *niños son muy traviesos.*

2. Match the following words to its English translation:
   a. el equipaje de mano i. the panties
   b. la playera ii. the shorts
   c. la sudadera iii. the flip-flops
   d. los pantalones cortos iv. the shirt
   e. las chancletas v. the sweatshirt
   f. las bragas vi. the carry-on luggage
3. Translate the following sentences into Spanish:
   a. "It's a quarter to three in the afternoon."
   b. "Excuse me, can you tell me the time, please?"
   c. "It's twenty past eight."
   d. "It's 1:30 p.m."
4. Are these words masculine or feminine?
   a. __ *toalla*
   b. __ *muelle*
   c. __ *protector solar*
   d. __ *hielera*
   e. __ *velero*
5. Complete the following sentences with the correct verb form in the present simple tense:
   a. *Yo _____ (hacer) surf cada verano* ("I practice surfing every year")
   b. *¡Yo _____ (traer) la pelota de playa!* ("I bring the beach ball!")
   c. *Yo me _____ (poner) la sudadera* ("I put on my hoodie")
   d. *Yo le _____ (dar) dinero al vendedor* ("I give money to the salesman")
   e. *Yo no _____ (saber) dónde está el muelle* ("I don't know where the pier is")
   f. *Yo _____ (conducir) hacia la playa* ("I drive towards the beach")

g. *Tú* _____ *(build) un castillo de arena* ("You build a sandcastle")
h. *Ella* _____ *(dormir) a la sombra* ("She sleeps in the shade")
i. *¿Qué* _____ *(pensar)?* ("What do you think?")
j. *Ellos* _____ *(pedir) un helado* ("they order an ice-cream")

Domingo: The Last Day

Sunday finally came, the day I was dreading. It was my last day of vacation before heading back home. I was having an incredible time and didn't want it to end. Paula had opened the doors to her home and had shown me the wonders of Mexico, and it was as if I had always lived here when I walked by her side. Of course, I was still a *güero* and a gringo, but that didn't stop me from getting to know the locals' way of life.

I only had less than 24 hours left to walk around Mexico City, but I was exhausted from the field trip on Saturday, so I didn't want to have a hectic day, to be honest. Paula suggested we had breakfast in a cafe she usually went to, so she picked me up, and we went on foot.

Plans for The Future (*futuro simple*)

Even though *carpe diem* was the mindset I had been practicing throughout this trip, I couldn't help but wonder about my future. What would it be in store for me when I returned from Mexico? Would my old life be as satisfying as when I hopped on the plane a week back?

When I expressed my concerns to Paula at the cafe, she told me to look at my horoscope on a local newspaper lying around.

"You better be joking," I replied. "You know horoscopes are just a made-up thing a journalist has to write for a living, right?"

"Of course I do, Georgie!" said Paula with a big smile. "But that doesn't mean we can't have a little fun, can't we? Come on, don't be a buzzkill."

She was right: there was no harm in joking around with those predictions. Besides, I could practice some of my reading comprehension in Spanish. I grabbed the newspaper and looked for the section called *Horóscopo semanal*. These were some of the predictions:
- Aries (21 de marzo-20 de abril). Una persona de tu pasado **volverá** a tu vida.
- Tauro (21 de abril-20 de mayo). **Recibirás** una buena noticia que te **pondrá** feliz.
- Géminis (21 de mayo-20 de junio). **Tendrás** algunos problemas en tu trabajo.
- Cáncer (21 de junio-20 de julio). El amor **tocará** tu puerta.
- Leo (21 de julio-20 de agosto). La suerte **estará** de tu lado.

Paula helped me translate them:
- Aries (March 21-April 20). A person from your past **will return** to your life.
- Taurus (April 21-May 20). You **will receive** good news that **will make** you happy.
- Gemini (May 21-June 20). You **will have** some problems at work.
- Cancer (June 21-July 20). Love **will knock** on your door.
- Leo (July 21-August 20). Luck **will be** on your side.

After reading, I noticed the verbs differed from those I had learned the previous days. Paula told me it was because they were in the future simple tense, which is called *el futuro simple* in Spanish. This tense is used to discuss future events and predictions (that's why the horoscope had so many of these verbs!). For the regular verbs, Paula told me I only had to add specific endings at the end of a verb in its bare form, but without taking anything out. She helped me learn the different endings there are for the *futuro simple* by using the verb *viajar*:
- *Yo viajaré*
- *Tú viajarás*
- *Usted viajará*
- *Él viajará*
- *Ella viajará*
- *Nosotros viajaremos*

- *Nosotras viajar**emos***
- *Ustedes viajar**án***
- *Ellos viajar**án***
- *Ellas viajar**án***

The endings É, ÁS, Á, EMOS, and ÁN are added at the end of the infinitive to make it a future tense.

"Tell me..." I said with hesitation. "There are exceptions to this rule, I presume?"

"How did you know?" replied Paula with a cheeky smile. "Of course, there are exceptions to this rule, but not regarding the endings. These ones stay the same no matter the type of conjugation. However, there are some irregular verbs that experience little changes in their roots..."

This is a list of the irregular verbs Paula mentioned:

- **Decir** ("to say"): *Yo diré la verdad* ("I will say the truth")
- **Hacer** ("to do"): *Yo haré mi trabajo* ("I will do my job")
- **Poder** ("can" or "to be able"): *Yo podré trabajar* ("I will be able to work")
- **Poner** ("to put"): *Yo pondré dinero en el banco* ("I will put money in the bank")
- **Querer** ("to love" or "to want"): *Yo te querré siempre* ("I will love you always")
- **Saber** ("to know"): *Yo sabré la respuesta* ("I will know the answer")
- **Salir** ("to go out"): *Yo saldré esta noche* ("I will go out tonight")
- **Tener** ("to have"): *El año que viene yo tendré dinero* ("Next year I will have money")
- **Venir** ("to come"): *Mañana vendré a verte* ("Tomorrow I will come see you")

"There are verbs which are more irregular than others," said Paula.

Paula also taught me the full conjugation for the verb *ser* in the *futuro simple:*

- Yo ser**é**
- *Tú* ser**ás**
- *Usted* ser**á**

- *Él será*
- *Ella será*
- *Nosotros ser**emos***
- *Nosotras ser**emos***
- *Ustedes ser**án***
- *Ellos ser**án***
- *Ellas ser**án***

Future Time Expressions

Paula thought I should know some time expressions to use with the *futuro simple* tense:

- *Ahorita* ("now" with both present and future meanings. This is a very common word in Mexico)
- *Mañana* ("tomorrow")
- *Mañana por la mañana* ("tomorrow morning")
- *Pasado mañana* ("the day after tomorrow")
- *El sábado que viene* ("next Saturday")
- *Dentro de un mes* ("within a month")
- *En un año* ("in a year")
- *Pronto* ("soon")
- *Eventualmente* ("eventually")
- *Más tarde* ("later")

Jobs and Professions

After focusing on the future tense, Paula thought it would be a good idea to skim through the newspaper (el periódico) a bit more. The section *ofertas laborales* caught my eye. Paula said this meant "job advertisements." I wasn't looking for a job or anything, but I realized I didn't know how to say my profession (programmer) in Spanish! My friend gave me a helping hand by telling me the Spanish version of some basic work vocabulary:

- *El trabajo* ("the job")
- *El empleo* ("the employment")
- *La profesión* ("the profession")

- *El oficio* ("the craft")

I appreciated those words, but I was curious to know more! That's why Paula pointed out the different jobs in the newspaper and taught me some extra ones with their male and female versions. Some female workers' names stay the same, and the only thing that changes is the gender of the definite article before the word. However, other professions also require either adding an A at the end of the word or changing the final O for an A. Here's a really long list of the professions:

- *El policía, la policía* ("the police officer")
- *El bombero, la bombera* ("the firefighter")
- *El abogado, la abogada* ("the lawyer")
- *El juez, la jueza* ("the judge")
- *El cartero, la cartera* ("the postal worker")
- *El doctor, la doctora / El médico, la médica* ("the doctor")
- *El enfermero, la enfermera* ("the nurse")
- *El farmacéutico, la farmacéutica* ("the pharmacist")
- *El cirujano, la cirujana* ("the surgeon")
- *El psicólogo, la psicóloga* ("the psychologist")
- *El programador, la programadora* ("the programmer")
- *El científico, la científica* ("the scientist")
- *El oficinista, la oficinista* ("the office worker")
- *El empresario, la empresaria* ("the businessperson")
- *El emprendedor, la emprendedora* ("the entrepreneur")
- *El recepcionista, la recepcionista* ("the receptionist")
- *El secretario, la secretaria* ("the secretary")
- *El asistente, la asistente* ("the assistant")
- *El escritor, la escritora* ("the writer")
- *El periodista, la periodista* ("the journalist")
- *El cantante, la cantante* ("the singer")
- *El bailarín, la bailarina* ("the dancer")
- *El pintor, la pintora* ("the painter")
- *El peluquero, la peluquera* ("the hairstylist")
- *El maquillador, la maquilladora* ("the makeup artist")

- *El tatuador, la tatuadora* ("the tattoo artist")
- *El diseñador, la diseñadora* ("the designer")
- *El arquitecto, la arquitecta* ("the architect")
- *El ingeniero, la ingeniera* ("the engineer")
- *El albañil, la albañil* ("the bricklayer")
- *El carpintero, la carpintera* ("the carpenter")
- *El plomero, la plomera* ("the plumber")
- *El herrero, la herrera* ("the blacksmith")
- *El electricista, la electricista* ("the electrician")
- *El mecánico, la mecánica* ("the mechanic")
- *El portero, la portera* ("the doorman" or "the doorwoman")
- *El casero, la casera* ("the landlord" or "the landlady")
- *El camionero, la camionera* ("the truck driver")
- *El taxista, la taxista ("the taxi driver")*
- *El conductor, la conductora / El chofer, la chofer* ("the driver" or "the chauffeur")
- *El campesino, la campesina* ("the farm worker")
- *El granjero, la granjera* ("the farmer")
- *El jardinero, la jardinera* ("the gardener")
- *El pescador, la pescadora* ("the fisherman" or "the fisherwoman")
- *El veterinario, la veterinaria* ("the vet")
- *El maestro, la maestra* ("the teacher")
- *El profesor, la profesora* ("the professor")
- *El economista, la economista* ("the economist")
- *El contador, la contadora* ("the accountant")
- *El cajero, la cajera* ("the cashier")
- *El comerciante, la comerciante* ("the merchant")
- *El conserje, la conserje* ("the janitor")
- *El trabajador del hogar, la trabajadora del hogar* ("the housekeeper")
- *El amo de casa, la ama de casa* ("full time dad" or "full time mom")

Luckily for me, some jobs had a very similar name to the words I used in English, so they were easy to remember. Then, Paula taught me some common questions and phrases regarding jobs:
- *¿A qué te dedicas?* ("What do you do?")
- *¿De qué trabajas?* ("What do you do for a living")
- *¿Cuál es tu trabajo?* ("What is your job?")
- *Trabajo como programador / Trabajo de programador* ("I work as a programmer")
- *Soy programador* ("I am a programmer")

The Past Tense (*pretérito perfecto simple*)

I was so confident with my Spanish level after that lesson. Paula congratulated me for my progress and asked if I was ready to learn a more advanced topic: the past tense.

"But haven't we learned the *pretérito imperfecto* yet?" I asked.

"We sure did, but there are other past tenses apart from the *pretérito imperfecto...*" said Paula with suspense. "I'm talking about the *pretérito perfecto simple*, a really important and common tense in Spanish."

According to Paula, the English past simple can be expressed with two different Spanish tenses: the *pretérito imperfecto* (which I'd already learned) and the *pretérito perfecto simple*. This new tense is also known as *pretérito indefinido*. Not only do these tenses have different grammatical expressions, but also different functions and meanings. *Pretérito imperfecto* is used to talk about past habits, routines, or emotions. Conversely, the *pretérito perfecto simple* is used in Spanish to talk about specific past actions, with a clear beginning and ending. For example, we can say *Ayer comí una manzana* ("Yesterday I ate an apple"). The verb *comí* comes from the verb *comer*, and describes an action that started and finished in a specific moment in the past.

"Does this tense need to be in agreement with the noun's person and number?" I asked.

"That's right," answered Paula. "Every personal pronoun has a specific ending and we also need to consider the different conjugations."

I was starting to get dizzy with so much information, but Paula tried to explain everything as simply as possible.

Regular Verbs Ending in AR

In order to conjugate verbs from the *primera conjugación* in the *pretérito perfecto simple*, first we need to take a verb in its infinitive form, like *trabajar* ("to work"), and remove the AR ending. After we obtain the root of the verb (*trabaj*), we need to add the following endings (I highlighted them in bold):

- Yo *trabaj***é**
- *Tú trabaj***aste**
- *Usted trabaj***ó**
- *Él trabaj***ó**
- *Ella trabaj***ó**
- *Nosotros trabaj***amos**
- *Nosotras trabaj***amos**
- *Ustedes trabaj***aron**
- *Ellos trabaj***aron**
- *Ellas trabaj***aron**

In other words, for the pronoun **yo**, we need to drop the AR ending and add an **É**.

For **tú**, we have to drop the AR ending and add **ASTE**.

For **usted**, **él**, and **ella**, we drop the AR ending and add an **Ó**.

Then, for **nosotros** and **nosotras**, we need to drop the AR ending and add **AMOS** (this ending is just like the one for the present simple tense!)

Finally, for **ustedes**, **ellos** and **ellas**, we drop the AR ending and add **ARON**.

Regular Verbs Ending in ER and IR

I was starting to get worried about the amount of new information, but luckily Paula told me the second and third conjugations use the same endings! She proceeded to give some examples with the verbs *comer* and *subir* ("to eat" and "to go up" respectively):

- Yo com**í** / Yo sub**í**
- *Tú com***iste** / *Tú sub***iste**
- *Usted com***ió** / *Usted sub***ió**
- *Él com***ió** / *Él sub***ió**
- *Ella com***ió** / *Ella sub***ió**

- *Nosotros com**imos** / Nosotros sub**imos***
- *Nosotras com**imos** / Nosotras sub**imos***
- *Ustedes com**ieron** / Ustedes sub**ieron***
- *Ellos com**ieron** / Ellos sub**ieron***
- *Ellas com**ieron** / Ellas sub**ieron***

By seeing this list of verbs, I understood that, for the pronoun *yo*, we need to drop the AR ending and add an **Í**.

For *tú*, we have to drop the AR ending and add **ISTE**.

For *usted*, *él,* and *ella*, we drop the AR ending and add an **Ó** (just like the first conjugation!).

Then, for **nosotros** and **nosotras**, we need to drop the AR ending and add **IMOS**.

Finally, for **ustedes**, **ellos** and **ellas**, we drop the AR ending and add **IERON**.

Irregular Verbs

As I predicted, some rebellious irregular verbs follow their unique rules. Because Paula didn't want to overwhelm me, she taught me the most common ones. She started with the verb *ser*, which had FU as its root:

- *Yo f**ui***
- *Tú f**uiste***
- *Usted f**ue***
- *Él f**ue***
- *Ella f**ue***
- *Nosotros fu**imos***
- *Nosotras fu**imos***
- *Ustedes fu**eron***
- *Ellos fu**eron***
- *Ellas fu**eron***

"*Fui?*" I asked in quite a shock. "*yo soy, yo era...* and now *yo fui?* This is too much!"

"Don't be such a *llorón!*," said Paula with a laugh (llorón means "crybaby"). "Your past simple irregular verbs are not so easy to learn either! 'To be' can be 'am,' 'is,' 'are,' 'was,, 'were,' AND 'been'? If I managed to learn your English irregular verbs; you can definitely learn the Spanish ones."

After that little scolding, Paula continued with the verb *ir*. Thankfully, she told me that **ir and ser shared the exact same past conjugation in the past simple!** That means that "I was" and "I went" can both be translated as *Yo fui*. So interesting!

"But how on earth am I going to be able to recognize which action they are talking about if they are the same in Spanish?" I asked Paula.

"Oh, you don't have to worry about that," she replied. "You'll most likely get it through context; it's not that difficult."

Then, Paula taught me the conjugation of *estar*. Sadly, even though it also means "to be," its root and endings are quite different. The root is ESTUV and the endings are the following ones:

- *Yo estuve*
- *Tú estuviste*
- *Usted estuvo*
- *Él estuvo*
- *Ella estuvo*
- *Nosotros estuvimos*
- *Nosotras estuvimos*
- *Ustedes estuvieron*
- *Ellos estuvieron*
- *Ellas estuvieron*

After that, she taught me two other very common irregular verbs: *hacer* ("to do") and *tener* ("to have").

For *hacer,* the endings are the same ones the verb *estar* uses, but the root is a bit more complicated. For seven out of ten possible pronouns, the root is HIC, but *usted, él* and *ella* have the following root: HIZ, with a Z. This is because, in Spanish, the vowels E and I cannot come after a Z, so we have to replace this consonant with a C when that happens. This is the case of the word *juez* ("judge"): its plural form is *jueces*, with a C, because of the vowel E. This is the conjugation for *hacer:*

- *Yo hice*
- *Tú hiciste*
- *Usted hizo*

- *Él hizo*
- *Ella hizo*
- *Nosotros hic**imos***
- *Nosotras hic**imos***
- *Ustedes hic**ieron***
- *Ellos hic**ieron***
- *Ellas hic**ieron***

Then, Paula told me the conjugation for *tener*:
- Yo *tuve*
- *Tú tuv**iste***
- *Usted tuvo*
- *Él tuvo*
- *Ella tuvo*
- *Nosotros tuv**imos***
- *Nosotras tuv**imos***
- *Ustedes tuv**ieron***
- *Ellos tuv**ieron***
- *Ellas tuv**ieron***

Paula told me I could look up the conjugation of other irregular verbs as I saw fit, depending on what I wanted to say.

Chapter Summary

After that coffee chat, we finished the day by wandering through the city and buying souvenirs for my family. As I had a hard time wrapping my head around everything I had learned that day, Paula helped me summarize all the grammar and vocabulary topics:

- First of all, we saw the *futuro simple* and its endings (É, ÁS, Á, EMOS and ÁN), as well as some irregular verbs we could encounter.
- Second of all, we focused on some future time expressions to use alongside the *futuro simple*.
- Then, we learned plenty of vocabulary regarding the professional field and its male and female versions.

- Finally, we dove head-first into the *pretérito perfecto simple*, which is used to talk about specific actions that began and ended in a specific moment in the past. We saw the different endings for each conjugation:
    - *Primera conjugación:* É, ASTE, Ó, AMOS and ARON.
    - *Segunda y tercera conjugación:* Í, ISTE, Ó, IMOS and IERON.
    - We also saw some common irregular verbs like *ser, estar, ir, hacer* and *tener.*

Cultural Annex

Paula told me that, in order to understand the Mexican way of live, I had to familiarize with some of their popular sayings:

- ***A quien lo quiere celeste, que le cueste*** ("Whoever wants it light blue, let it cost them"). This saying implies that in order to achieve something (like painting something in light blue), you have to put in the work (that is, mixing blue and white, for example).
- ***El flojo trabaja dos veces*** ("The slacker works twice"). This phrase condemns laziness and says that a lazy person must put in twice the work as a good worker in order to achieve the same results.
- ***Al que madruga, Dios lo ayuda*** ("Whoever gets up early, God will help them"). This saying celebrates early birds and says that luck will be on their side. There is an English equivalent to this saying: "The early bird catches the worm."
- ***No dejes para mañana lo que puedes hacer hoy*** ("Don't leave until tomorrow what you can do today"). This saying is quite self-explanatory, for it criticizes procrastination.

Exercises

1. Translate the following phrases into Spanish (don't forget to contemplate both possible genders):
    a. "I will be a teacher."
    b. "She works as a hairstylist."
    c. "They are bricklayers."

2. Match the following words to its English translation:
    a. el plomero   i. the writer
    b. el oficio   ii. the plumber
    c. la escritora   iii. the craft
    d. la médica   iv. the doctor
3. Write the whole conjugation for the verb *ser* in the *futuro simple* and in the *pretérito imperfecto*.
4. Are the following sentences correct? Correct the wrong ones:
    a. *¿A qué trabajas?*
    b. *¿Trabajas como oficinista?*
    c. *Carlos es periodisto.*
5. Decide whether the following statement is true or false. If it's false, correct it.

    In the *pretérito perfecto simple,* the verbs *ser* and *estar* share the same meaning and conjugation.

Time to Go Home

Finally, the time had come for me to head back home to LA. Mexico had blown my mind in ways I didn't think possible, and I was sad to leave. I was especially distraught to say goodbye to Paula. My friend had been by my side every step of my Spanish journey, and she had opened my eyes to a whole different culture. While driving to the airport, I kept thinking about all that Paula had taught me, and I couldn't help imagining myself speaking Spanish in other countries, like Spain. When I told Paula what I was daydreaming about, she gave me a warning:

"You do know Spanish changes quite a lot between countries, right? Imagine yourself talking to a Scotsman; you would have a hard time understanding some things!"

"But... What can be so different between Mexican Spanish and the Spanish spoken in Spain?" I asked.

"Well, if you want to know, there are three key aspects to remember: pronunciation, grammar and vocabulary. We don't have much time, so I'll only stick to the basics."

Pronunciation Differences: *Seseo*

For starters, Paula reminded me that, in Mexican Spanish, Z is pronounced like S every time. **The lack of distinction between "s," "c" and "z" is called *seseo*,** and it's a common trait in Latin America.

However, **in Spain, Z has a sound similar to English TH in "think." That sound can be represented with the symbol θ.** For example, if we compare the words *casa* and *caza* ("house" and "hunting" respectively), in Mexico, they would be pronounced the same way, with an S sound: /kasa/ and /kasa/. In Spain, on the other hand, *casa* would be pronounced /kasa/, and *caza* would be /kaθa/, sticking out the tip of the tongue between your teeth, like the English TH in "think."

This θ sound can also appear when the letter C comes before the vowels E and I, like in the words *césped* and *cielo* ("grass" and "sky" respectively).

Grammar Differences: *Ustedes* vs *Vosotros*

After I understood the pronunciation differences, Paula told me about the different pronouns Spaniards use. Whereas Latin American Spanish uses *ustedes* as its second-person plural pronoun ("you" in English), European Spanish has two different pronouns: **vosotros** and **vosotras**. *Vosotras* is used to address a group of only feminine subjects, whereas *vosotros* is used to address both a group of all-male subjects and a group with masculine and feminine subjects (like the male-as-norm principle tells us).

"That isn't so bad..." I said.

"Hold on now," interrupted Paula. "There's a catch: not only do we need to change the pronouns, but also the conjugation!"

Paula explained that *ustedes* has a different conjugation than *vosotros/vosotras*. She told me to review the endings *ustedes* has with the three example verbs, *amar*, *temer*, and *partir*:

	1°: am**ar** ("to love")	*2°*: tem**er** ("to fear")	*3°*: part**ir** ("to leave")
Presente simple	Ustedes am**an**	Ustedes tem**en**	Ustedes part**en**
Pretérito imperfecto	Ustedes am**aban**	Ustedes tem**ían**	Ustedes part**ían**
Pretérito perfecto simple	Ustedes am**aron**	Ustedes tem**ieron**	Ustedes part**ieron**

| Futuro simple | Ustedes am**arán** | Ustedes tem**erán** | Ustedes part**irán** |

After that recap, Paula asked me to make another table with the same information, but this time she would tell me the different endings for *vosotros/as*. One of the main differences here is that, whereas *ustedes* and *ellos/as* share the same conjugation in Mexican Spanish, Spaniard Spanish has its own distinct conjugation for *vosotros/as*.

	1°: am**ar** ("to love")	*2°*: tem**er** ("to fear")	*3°*: part**ir** ("to leave")
Presente simple	Vosotros/as am**áis**	Vosotros/as tem**éis**	Vosotros/as part**ís**
Pretérito imperfecto	Vosotros/as am**abais**	Vosotros/as tem**íais**	Vosotros/as part**íais**
Pretérito perfecto simple	Vosotros/as am**asteis**	Vosotros/as tem**isteis**	Vosotros/as part**isteis**
Futuro simple	Vosotros/as am**aréis**	Vosotros/as tem**eréis**	Vosotros/as part**iréis**

Vocabulary Differences: Indigenisms and Mexicanisms

When we arrived at the airport, Paula stood in line with me as I went through customs. During that waiting period, she explained the third key aspect of why Mexican Spanish differs so much from Spaniard Spanish. When Hernán Cortés traveled in the 16th century to the land now called Mexico, he encountered many ancient tribes who had lived there for centuries. Not only did he encounter the Aztec civilization at Tenochtitlan, but he also learned *Nahuatl*, the natives' language in Mexico. There were more languages, of course, but Nahuatl was the most influential one, and it can be found today in the names of regions like Acapulco, Jalapa, Jalisco... Even Mexico is a *nahua* name! Nahuatl is still very much alive today, and it's spoken by around three million people.

After the Spanish conquistadors took control of the Central American area, they kept Nahuatl as the lingua franca, a language that would help them communicate with other native tribes apart from Spanish. As a logical consequence of this language clash between the Spaniards and the Americans, Spanish has then been enriched thanks to this "lexical treasure." The process of naming all the objects of this "New World" started with the use of European names: for example, they called the jaguar "tiger," the hummingbird "sparrow," and so on. However, this became insufficient pretty soon, and Spaniards started incorporating indigenous names into their language. Thanks to this mixture of languages and cultures, the American continent has hundreds of variants of Spanish, very different from that of its European "father."

These loanwords from Nahuatl can be found in Mexican Spanish today. Spaniards kept only that name when they were used to name something that didn't exist in Europe. Nonetheless, in Spain, they still use words that are different from those we have in Mexico, which already existed at the time of the Conquest and share the same meaning as their American versions.

At this point in Paula's explanation, I was ready to enter the boarding area. She could no longer join me, so it was time to say goodbye. We melted in a big and strong hug.

"I'm going to miss you, Georgie," said Paula. "You may be a *gringo güero*, but know that Mexico will always be your second home and that you're always welcome in my home."

"Thank you, my *amiga*," I replied with a knot in my throat. "This was the best experience of my life. I'm going to miss you terribly. *Mi casa es tu casa* too in the US. *Hasta pronto*, see you soon!"

Of course, Paula couldn't let me go without giving me two charts, one with a list of words derived from Nahuatl and another filled with Mexicanisms. As the escalator drew me away from my friend, I became emotional. I knew I would see her again, but I was still too moved by this whole experience.

During takeoff, I looked out the window and stared at *la Ciudad de México* as it became smaller and smaller. Right after leaving that lovely city behind, I took out Paula's charts from my carry-on and started reading them.

Mexican Words Derived from Nahuatl

In this first chart, there was a list of Mexican words derived from Nahuatl. I saw that some of the cells from the European Spanish equivalents were empty because some of the words are used in both dialects.

Mexican Spanish words derived from Nahuatl	English translation	European Spanish equivalent (if any)
el aguacate	avocado	-
el jitomate	tomato	*el tomate*
el cacahuate	peanut	*el cacahuete*
el chocolate	chocolate	-
el cacao	cocoa	-
el elote	corn, maize ear	*el maíz*
el guajolote	turkey	*el pavo*
el cuate, la cuata	friend	*el/la colega, el tío/la tía*
el chicle	gum	-
el popote	straw	*la pajilla*
la tiza	chalk	-

Mexicanisms

After studying the first chart, I moved over to the list of Spanish Mexicanisms. According to Paula, Nahuatl is not the only influence in

Mexican Spanish: some factors include other indigenous languages, "archaisms" (words that were common in Spain in the past but now are not), and even words from English because of how close Mexico and the United States are located.

Mexicanisms	English translation	European Spanish equivalent (if any)
las agujetas	shoelaces	*los cordones*
la alberca	pool	*la piscina*
el antro	bar	*el bar*
la banqueta	sidewalk	*la acera*
el camarón	shrimp	*la gamba*
el camión	bus	*el autobús*
el carro	car	*el coche*
el celular	cellphone	*el móvil*
el chamaco, la chamaca	kid	*el chaval, la chavala*
la chamarra	jacket	*la chaqueta*
chambear	to work	*trabajar*
la chela	beer	*la cerveza*
la colonia	neighborhood (specially in Mexico City)	*el barrio*

Mexicanisms	English translation	European Spanish equivalent (if any)
la cruda	hangover	*la resaca*
la feria	extra change, quarters	*la calderilla, la chatarra*
fregar	to annoy	*fastidiar*
el güero, la güera	blond	*el rubio, la rubia*
el güey	guy, dude	*el tío, el colega*
el huarache	sandals	*la sandalia*
la lana	money	*el dinero, la plata*
el lonche	lunch, sandwich	*el almuerzo, el sándwich*
el mesero, la mesera	waiter	*el camarero, la camarera*
la neta	truth	*la verdad*
padrísimo/a	great, amazing	*increíble, muy bueno*
el pasto	grass	*el césped*
platicar	to talk	*hablar, conversar*
el platillo	dish	*el plato*

Mexicanisms	English translation	European Spanish equivalent (if any)
la playera	t-shirt	*la camiseta*
el refrigerador	fridge	*la nevera*
la soda, el refresco	soda	*la gaseosa*
la torta	sandwich	*el sándwich, el bocadillo*
los tenis	sneakers	*las zapatillas*
las zapatillas	high heels	*los zapatos de tacón*

After I read the last word, I realized I would no longer have Paula at my side to help me learn Spanish, and that thought made me sad. However, I quickly understood that was not true: as long as I learned Spanish, I could always contact her and ask her something about the language; this would be an excellent excuse to catch up.

While putting away the charts, the old woman beside me asked me if I was learning Spanish. When I told her I was, she became emotional: forty years ago, her American husband started learning Spanish to conquer her heart, which he most definitely did. From that moment on, they lived happily ever after, even though she wasn't good at speaking English. Their love was the binding force that kept them together. Her story really moved me, so I suggested we talk in Spanish. She was ecstatic! We then proceeded to talk for hours. We didn't chat about the meaning of life or anything as complicated as that, but with patience, I could express myself and understand her quite a bit. I was beyond myself: I was conversing in Spanish with a native speaker! I couldn't wait to text Paula after I landed in LA.

Three and a half hours later, with my head filled with knowledge and my heart filled with joy, I waited for the plane to land. And with that nice end to my holidays, I continued studying Spanish until today.

Answer Key

Chapter 1: *lunes*

1.
   - a. *¿Cuál es tu nombre?*
   - b. *Yo soy Mara, ¿quién eres tú?*
   - c. *¿Cómo estás?*
   - 2. *Mi nombre es Sara.*
   - 3. *Yo soy Luis.*
   - 1. *Bien, ¿y tú?*

2. False. The "generic masculine" designates the capacity of the masculine grammatical gender to name a group of both men and women.

3.
   Person 1: **Hola**, *yo* **soy** *Alejandro. ¿Quién eres* **tú***?*
   Person 2: *Mucho* **gusto***, Alejandro. Yo soy Nelly. ¿Cómo* **estás***?*
   Person 2: *Muy bien,* **gracias***.*

4.
   - b. *Tú* is informal and the *usted* is formal.

5. False. In Spanish, all regular verbs of a given conjugation undergo the same changes when we conjugate them.

Chapter 2: *martes*

1.
   - a. *Modernas*
   - b. *Viejas*
   - c. *Moradas*
   - d. *Negras*
   - e. *Pequeñas*

2. False. In Spanish, adjectives usually go after the noun they are modifying.

3.
   - a. *El comedor*, feminine: *la mesa*
   - b. *La sala*, feminine: *la alfombra*
   - c. *El baño*, feminine: *la toalla*
   - d. *La cocina*, masculine: *el fuego*
   - e. *El baño*, masculine: *el espejo*

4. Translate the following sentences from English to Spanish:
   - a. *La mesa es vieja.*
   - b. *Hay una silla vieja y verde / Hay una silla verde y vieja.*
   - c. *El refrigerador está en la cocina.*

5.
   b. In the present simple tense, the verb *haber* can be used only in the third-person singular form.

Chapter 3: *miércoles*

1. How do you say eighty four in Spanish?
   - d. *Ochenta y cuatro*

2.
   - a. *Primo segundo* — 3. Second cousin
   - b. *Familia monoparental* — 1. Single-parent family
   - c. *Yerno* — 2. Son in law

3. False. In Spanish, possessive pronouns have to agree in gender and number with the person who possesses the object and with the object.

4. All three sentences were incorrect.
   a. *Ella es **mí** prima.*
   b. *Yo **tengo** ocho hermanos.*
   c. *¿Él es **su** abuelo?*
5.
   a. *Yo tengo ... hermanos y ... hermanas.*
   b. *Mi madre tiene ... años de edad.*
   c. *Yo tengo ... tíos y ... tías.*

Chapter 4: *jueves*

1.
   a. El *desayuno* / *Desayunar*
   b. *El almuerzo* / *Almorzar*
   c. *La merienda* / *Merendar*
   d. *La cena* / *Cenar*
2.
   a. *el jitomate, la lechuga, la cebolla*
   b. *el tenedor, el cuchillo, la cuchara*
   c. *el pollo, el pescado, la ternera*
3. False: In Spanish, in order to ask for the check, you can say the following: *La cuenta, por favor.*
4. All the sentences were incorrect.
   a. *Tengo **una** reserva para dos personas a nombre de Gutiérrez.*
   b. *¿Cuál es el menú **del día**?*
   c. *¿Puedo **envolver** esto para llevar?*
   d. ***Estamos** listos para pedir.*
5. *Ponerle mucha crema a los tacos.*

Chapter 5: *viernes*

1. *Un, una, unos, unas, algún, alguna, algunos, algunas*
2.
    a. *el ayuntamiento* — iii. the city hall
    b. *la avenida principal* — ii. the main avenue
    c. *la iglesia* — i. the church
    d. *la fuente* — iv. the fountain
3. *Yo voy, tú vas, usted va, él va, ella va, nosotros vamos, nosotras vamos, ustedes van, ellos van, ellas van*

    Yo iba, tú ibas, usted iba, él iba, ella iba, nosotros íbamos, nosotras íbamos, ustedes iban, ellos iban, ellas iban
4. Sentences a and c are incorrect and sentence b is correct.

    a. *¿**Cómo** llego al cine?*
    b. *¿El parque está lejos?*
    c. *¿Podría decirme cómo ir al museo, **por favor**?*
5. False: in the *pretérito imperfecto*, these are the endings that correspond to the first conjugation: ABA, ABAS, ÁBAMOS and ABAN.

Chapter 6: *sábado*

1.
    a. ***Aquel***: demonstrative adjective, far from both.
    b. ***Esta***: demonstrative pronoun, close to the speaker.
    c. ***Eso***: demonstrative pronoun, close to the addressee.
    d. ***Estos***: demonstrative adjective, close to the speaker.
2.
    a. *el equipaje de mano* — vi. the carry-on
    b. *la playera* — iv. the t-shirt
    c. *la sudadera* — ii. the hoodie
    d. *los pantalones cortos* — i. the shorts
    e. *las chancletas* — iii. the flip flops
    f. *las bragas* — v. the panties

3.
   a. *Son las tres menos cuarto de la tarde*
   b. *Disculpe, ¿puede por favor decirme la hora?*
   c. *Son las ocho y veinte*
   d. *Es la una y media de la tarde*

4.
   a. **la** *toalla* (feminine)
   b. **el** *muelle* (masculine)
   c. **el** *protector solar* (masculine)
   d. **la** *hielera* (feminine)
   e. **el** *velero* (masculine)

5.
   a. *Yo* **hago** *surf cada verano*
   b. *¡Yo* **traigo** *la pelota de playa!*
   c. *Yo me* **pongo** *la sudadera*
   d. *Yo le* **doy** *dinero al vendedor*
   e. *Yo no* **sé** *dónde está el muelle*
   f. *Yo* **conduzco** *hacia la playa*
   g. *Tú* **construyes** *un castillo de arena*
   h. *Ella* **duerme** *a la sombra*
   i. *¿Qué* **piensas***?*
   j. *Ellos* **piden** *un helado*

Chapter 7: *domingo*

1.
   a. *Yo seré un maestro / Yo seré una maestra*
   b. *Ella trabaja como peluquera / Ella trabaja de peluquera*
   c. *Ellos son albañiles / Ellas son albañiles*

2.
   a. *el plomero*   ii. the plumber
   b. *el oficio*   iii. the craft
   c. *la escritora*   i. the writer
   d. *la médica*   iv. the doctor

3. *Yo seré, tú serás, usted será, él será, ella será, nosotros seremos, nosotras seremos, ustedes serán, ellos serán, ellas serán*

    Yo fui, tú fuiste, usted fue, él fue, ella fue, nosotros fuimos, nosotras fuimos, ustedes fueron, ellos fueron, ellas fueron

4. Sentences a and c are incorrect:

    a. *¿**De** qué trabajas?*

    c. *Carlos es periodis**ta**.*

5. False. In the *pretérito perfecto simple*, the verbs *ser and ir share the same conjugation but not the same meaning.*

Conclusion

¡*Buen trabajo!* What a fun ride this Mexican-Spanish journey has been. *¿Cómo estás, güey?* Do you feel all that Spanish knowledge flowing through your veins? I hope you do because you've been working so hard these last seven days as you followed George in his Mexican adventure.

Let's recap all you've learned while reading this Spanish language manual:

Before landing in *Ciudad de México*, George (and you) focused on Spanish pronunciation: vowel and consonant sounds.

El lunes, we saw George meet his friend Paula in Mexico City after a long time. As expected, our American friend (and you) started learning greetings and farewells, which included:

- different ways to greet someone, like **Hola**, **Buenos días** and **Bienvenido**
- ways of asking how someone is, with questions like **¿Cómo estás?** or **¿Qué tal?**;
- some possible answers to these questions, such as **Muy bien** or **Bien, ¿y tú?**;
- and farewell phrases, such as **Adiós**, **Adiosito** and **Hasta luego**.

Then, Paula taught you some phrases to introduce yourselves, like **Hola, yo soy George** and **Mucho gusto, George. Yo soy Paula.** You also learned about the ten personal pronouns in Spanish and how regular verbs are conjugated according to its type and the subject of said action. Finally, you saw how to conjugate the very irregular verb **ser** in the present simple tense.

El martes, you dove head first into home-related vocabulary, such as the parts of the house (*la sala, el comedor, el baño*) and all the different items of furniture you can find inside these rooms (*la mesa, la toalla, la almohada, el horno*). To use all of this vocabulary in a conversation, George and you had to learn two key verbs: *estar* and the impersonal *haber*. You also had to focus on fundamental grammar topics like Spanish gender and number and the definite articles *el, la, los,* and *las*. Finally, two other vocabulary topics were addressed:

- Common adjectives with their gender and number variations, like *pequeño/a/os/as* and *moderno/a/os/as*
- Colors, like *azul, rojo, blanco*, etc.

El miércoles, it was all about Paula's family as she opened the doors to her home and told George key vocabulary about:

- la familia cercana, like **la mamá, el papá** or **los hermanos**
- la familia extendida, like **los tíos, los cuñados** or **los suegros**
- los tipos de familia, like **la familia monoparental** or **la familia ensamblada**.

After that, Paula taught George and you about possessive adjectives (*mi, su, nuestras*...), pronouns (suyo, nuestro, mí...), and the numbers from *cero* to *cien*! In order to talk about family and numbers, this chapter included the irregular verb *tener*. Finally, Paula told George a short story about her family in Spanish for him to practice his listening skills.

El jueves, Paula took George out to dinner at a traditional Mexican restaurant, the perfect place to learn some interesting vocabulary about food, like *la servilleta, los cubiertos, la cena,* and different food and drinks, such as *el aguacate, el café,* etc. Then, George and Paula tasted some Mexican specialties, like *tacos, enchiladas, mole,* and many other delights. To top it off, George wrote down some useful phrases at a restaurant:

- *Tengo una reserva para dos personas.*
- *¿Cuál es el menú del día?*
- *¿Me pasarías la sal, por favor?*
- *La cuenta, por favor.*

El viernes, it was Paula and George's time to wander around Mexico City and visited several tourist attractions, such as **la catedral, el ayuntamiento** and **la fuente**, among others. To talk about movement, George learned the very irregular verb *ir*, and other actions like **caminar, entrar,** and **volver**. Then, George and you focused on asking for directions with the following phrases:

- ¿*Dónde está el puerto?*
- ¿*Podría decirme cómo llegar al puerto, por favor?*
- ¿*En qué calle está el puerto?*

After that, some other grammar topics covered in this chapter were the following:

- Indefinite articles, like **un, unas** and **algunos**
- Prepositions and adverbs of place, such as **lejos, cerca, entre,** etc.

Finally, Paula taught George about the *pretérito indefinido*, that past tense we use to talk about past habits, routines, or emotions. This was exemplified by a history leaflet that George found at a museum.

El sábado, it was time Paula and George went on a day trip to the beach! Before they left, George learned some interesting vocabulary about things one can find in their bag, like **el bañador, las chancletas** and **el protector solar**. Then, because they set off to the beach at such an early hour, Paula taught George and you how to tell the time with vocabulary like **la hora, los minutos,** and **aproximadamente**, and phrases like these:

- *Disculpe, ¿qué hora es?*
- *Perdona, ¿puedes decirme la hora, por favor?*
- ¿*A qué hora es el partido?*
- *Son las siete menos cuarto de la mañana*
- *Son las diez en punto de la mañana*
- *Son las doce y media del mediodía.*

After they arrived at the beach, Paula mentioned some interesting vocabulary words for things you could find in that scenario, like la sombrilla, la tumbona, la arena, and **las olas**. Even though it was a fun day under the sun, the Spanish lesson wasn't over just yet. Paula focused on demonstrative adjectives (**este, esos, aquellas**...) and pronouns (**esta, esas, aquel**...). Finally, the day ended with a very difficult topic: irregular

verbs in the present simple tense. Paula mentioned the irregularities that can be found within the apparent chaos and classified them into six groups:
- Group one: the first-person singular pronoun *yo* undergoes a change in its root, while all the other pronouns stay the same. This is the case for *yo* **hago** / **doy** / **sé** / **salgo**, etc.
- Group two: this affects verbs that end in a vowel + CIR/CER. Again, these verbs are only irregular when we conjugate them in the first-person: *yo* **traduzco** / **conduzco** / **conozco**, etc.
- Group three: verbs ending in UIR. To conjugate them with all pronouns except for *nosotros* and *nosotras*, we add a Y between the root and the ending, like *yo* **construyo** / **huyo**, etc.
- Group four: verbs that change an O of the root for UE, but otherwise follow the regular pattern. This is true for all pronouns except for the first-person plural *nosotros* and *nosotras*, which follow the regular pattern, like in *yo* **duermo** / **pruebo**.
- Group five: verbs with a vocalic change in the root, from an E to IE. Again, these changes apply to all pronouns except for *nosotros* and *nosotras*, like in *yo* **pienso** / **despierto**, etc.
- Group six: verbs that change an E in the infinitive to an I in the present. As with the previous changes, pronouns *nosotros* and *nosotras* maintain their root, like in *yo* **pido** / **visto**, etc.

El domingo, the last day, was a time to look back (with the pretérito perfecto simple) and forward (with the *futuro simple*). This future tense and its common endings (É, ÁS, Á, EMOS, and ÁN) were explained, and Paula gave examples of irregular verbs with a change of root: *yo* **vendré** / **saldré** / **querré**, etc. She also shared some future time expressions, such as **mañana**, **la semana que viene** and **pronto**. Then, George learned plenty of vocabulary about jobs and professions with their female versions, like **el médico/la médica** or **el periodista/la periodista**. Finally, the day ended with a difficult topic, which is the *pretérito perfecto simple,* a past tense to talk about specific actions that started and finished in a specific past moment. Of course, Paula taught George the regular endings for the first conjugation (É, ASTE, Ó, AMOS, ARON) and the ones for both the second and third conjugations (Í, ISTE, Ó, IMOS, IERON), and she finished it off with some common irregular verbs, such as *yo* **fui** / **estuve** / **tuve**, etc.

When the trip ended, George learned the differences between Mexican and Castilian Spanish and read some charts with some Mexican words derived from Nahuatl and some common Mexicanisms.

"What now?" you may ask. Well, it's time to keep on learning and practicing as much as you can! Each phrase you say and understand in Spanish is another step towards confidently achieving your goal of fluency.

¡*Vámonos!*

Here's another book by Lingo Publishing that you might like

Free Bonuses from Cecilia Melero

Hi Spanish Learners!

My name is Cecilia Melero, and first off, I want to THANK YOU for reading my book.

Now you have a chance to join my exclusive Spanish language learning email list so you can get the ebooks below for free as well as the potential to get more Spanish books for free! Simply click the link below to join.

P.S. Remember that it's 100% free to join the list.

Access your free bonuses here:
https://livetolearn.lpages.co/mexican-spanish-for-beginners-paperback/

www.ingramcontent.com/pod-product-compliance
Lightning Source LLC
Chambersburg PA
CBHW070335010526
44107CB00004B/518